DANTE AND OTHER WANING CLASSICS

DANTE AND OTHER WANING CLASSICS

Dante, Milton, Bunyan
A Kempis, St. Augustine, and Pascal

BY

ALBERT MORDELL

Author of *The Shifting of Literary Values*

KENNIKAT PRESS, INC./PORT WASHINGTON, N. Y.

CONTENTS

DANTE AND OTHER
WANING CLASSICS

PREFACE

I have chosen for critical examination six of the most famous classics of Christendom. These include two highly lauded epic poems of modern times, the *Divine Comedy* and *Paradise Lost;* two works the circulation of each of which has been surpassed only by the Bible, the *Imitation of Christ* and *Pilgrim's Progress;* a noted religious autobiography, St. Augustine's *Confessions* and an important product in Christian apologetics, Pascal's *Thoughts.* These works are saturated in whole or part with theological dogmas that have been discarded by many people to-day. It is my intention to show how medieval fallacies have ruined what might otherwise have been perfect literary masterpieces. The passages in these books that still live are the secular ones. These we can still read with enjoyment, but the authors regarded them as subsidiary to the theological intent. I have tried to point out that the literary value of these classics has waned in proportion to the extent and falsity of the theology pervading them.

Literature should not be a vehicle for theology. The poet often must describe sensations the theologian fears; he must express ideas the latter dare not think. Theology attaches itself usually to untenable and evanescent dogmas; its spirit is that of restraint; its atmosphere is confining. Literature shuns creeds and edicts and theories; it knows few barriers; it seeks the open. The chief mission of literature is often to undo the evil work wrought by false theologies. It is sublime when it depicts tragedies due to conformity with theological ethics. It is glorious when it shows us types who have emancipated themselves from tenets which enslave the mind and stifle the soul. Literature deals with realities, theology with illusions. One is the worship of beauty, grants deference to the senses, advocates liberality of speculation; the other means fig leaves and cramping garments, horror of the body and the natural emotions, enmity to daring investigation. The paths of literature and theology lie in opposite directions. One is ever seeking new truths, the other rests content with the old. One loves liberty, the other bows to authority; one breaks down idols, the other worships them. One is restless, ever questioning, ever animated; the other is passive, subscribing to some faith and chilled to the marrow.

Literature takes man as he is; it roots itself in human nature and material as well as spiritual desires; it shows us the individual with his impulses to exercise all his faculties and satisfy his instincts. Theology is taken up with devotion and repentance; it aims after piety; it wishes to dehumanize man.

" If literature is to be made a study of human nature," wrote Cardinal Newman, who certainly was no enemy of theology, "you cannot have a Christian literature. It is a contradiction in terms to attempt a sinless literature of sinful man."

It is a matter of great regret that some of the ablest writers should have embraced doctrines that have become obsolete. What a pity that the presence of exploded dogmas should vitiate literary performances! It is still sadder when we find that the entire substructures of some classics are founded on the fossilized remains of false principles.

It must be remembered that the great reputation attained by the classics I am examining, was originally created by literary guides who subscribed to the very doctrines which these works advocated. The favorable judgment was carried down to and repeated by succeeding critics who also adhered to the same dogmas. Finally when the foundations of these books were shaken, people continued to hold them in the greatest esteem, but found other reasons for doing so. We should not be misled into blindly worshipping literary productions with whose central ideas and views of life we totally disagree.

My attempt to dislodge these famous works from their high place no doubt seems presumptuous. They have the approval of the past behind them. It would be much easier to follow in the beaten track and add my share of praise. Moreover some one will certainly be offended. I have met people who admire Milton but are not moved by Dante. Some wax eloquent over Pascal but are horrified by A Kempis. However it will be seen that my effort is not always iconoclastic. I have tried to see value in many of the secular portions in these classics which æsthetic critics still admire. But I have thought it best to state my adverse views strongly when I felt justified. I also did not consider it necessary to engage in polemical work and try to demolish dogmas whose falsity I take for granted.

The principles of criticism I have applied have been laid down in a booklet I published several years ago called *The Shifting of Literary Values*. For reasons advanced there, I do not follow the rule that one should judge books by the times in which they were written, for historical criticism often tends to become an apology for past error; and I assume that the intellectual import of a book must also be taken into consideration apart from the technical qualities in it.

I also wish to state that it is not absolutely necessary that the reader should have read the various books here dealt with, in order to be able to pursue my argument. I have tried to give an outline of the plot or a summary of the leading ideas of the classics studied, in the course of my criticism. Undoubtedly, however, the person who is familiar with these works will be in a more advantageous position to pass upon the merits or demerits of my views.

It is a pleasure to me to be able to express my thanks and acknowledgments for encouragement, assistance and reading of the manuscript and proofs to my friends David Bortin, Esq., of the Philadelphia bar, and George Dobsevage, of New York.

ALBERT MORDELL.

August 13, 1915.

DANTE: THE DIVINE COMEDY

Dante is usually regarded one of the three greatest of the world's poets. The reader has the right to expect that his emotions will be aroused to their highest pitch by the poetical masterpiece of one who ranks so high. He is justified in assuming that he will not find his intelligence insulted too frequently and that the poem will possess much that is still vital to-day. He dare hope that he will not often see a display of bad taste, false judgments and unworthy sentiments. Indeed he should demand that a work of such great repute as the *Divine Comedy* should move him more than most literary productions do. The poem should be free from most of the intellectual errors and artistic deficiencies of other literary products of the time in which it was written; it should still make a strong appeal to us.

The reader has but to turn at random to a few cantos of the *Inferno* and of the *Paradiso* to discover immediately two facts about the poet. The first is that Dante delighted in contriving horrible and imaginary tortures in the next world for those who sinned here. The stern and vindictive Florentine heaps up the most revolting and nauseating horrors upon horrors; he has appointed himself moral censor of his fellow men and torments them with the most hideous punishments; he fails in the first function a poet should have, that of winning our sympathy. He alienates it from beginning to end, from the time he puts in the first circle of hell unbaptized infants and great men of Rome and Greece until he shows us in the last circle the fictitious Lucifer chewing in his mouth the Roman patriots Brutus and Cassius along with Judas. The second fact about the poet is that he follows the scholastic philosophy, and peoples his heaven chiefly with saints, theologians, crusaders and characters who subscribed to theological absurdities. Dante was a man of great learning but little intellect; he ignored vast treasures of ancient culture rediscovered prior to the Renaissance. He was hopelessly behind his own time in philosophy and religion; he was a serious adherent to dogmas and doctrines that many people were abandoning in his own day. No poem contains more versified hopeless speculation than the *Paradiso*. Much of this section is no longer considered of any æsthetic import and is studied by commentators who wish to know the beliefs entertained by the poet. From the very first canto where the universe is vaguely described as something like unto God, to the last where the poet actually tells us that he caught a glimpse of God Himself, we marvel as we read that his intellect was so limited. His power as a poet is corroded by his weakness as a thinker.

In the *Divine Comedy* we having living before us again all the bigotry and fatuity of the medieval ages; we have a summing up of all the speculation which rational men to-day reject; all the superstition, darkness and intolerance of a millennium are crystallized in this poem. But there are several episodes where the poet forgets his views and tells us of actual events of human interest; these stories usually proceed from the lips of different characters he meets in his sojourn and are the literary portions of the work that continue to live for us. They are the only passages that really give the *Divine Comedy* any poetical merit and have carried it forward into our time. The famous Paolo and Francesca story is one of these gems set in a heap of refuse matter. The poet's personality also interests us; his comments, his execrations, his hatred of moral infamy, his attitude toward friends and enemies he meets, all give us an insight into the soul of the unfortunate and proud Italian exile. We condemn and admire and pity and smile at him as we read on, but he has drawn his own portrait as if he had painted it on canvas for us.

Let us examine the poem as an artistic product. Let us lay stress on all the ugliness, grotesqueness and cruelty in it; let us not be hindered by the eulogies that have been pronounced upon it; let us disentangle the several fine episodes and declamations in it. We shall have as a residuum something that will still give the poet a place in literature, although not among the greatest of the world's poets. We shall discover that very few poets have been as much overrated as Dante, that he has scarcely any message for us and that the few ideas that he did try to convey to us were embodied in images that do not stir us. His chief merit will be found to reside in his reports of a few disconnected conversations held here and there by the poet with some character he meets in the other world. But interesting as some of these talks are they do not possess sufficient importance to entitle the poet to the wide repute and study he has received. It will be salutary to humanity if his fame declines and the Dante worship ceases. His reputation should not suffer the total eclipse that it experienced in the seventeenth and eighteenth centuries but civilization will profit if reactionary dogmatists will find that they can no longer appeal to his authority for their pernicious and obsolete views.

The *Inferno* has been the most popular of the three divisions of the *Divine Comedy*. It is picturesque and vivid,

even though inhuman and exotic.   Dante divides his hell into
nine circles whose gates are guarded by demons and mythological figures.   Each circle carries within it punishments
alleged to be fitting for the victims.   But as a matter of fact
the poor wretches in the first six circles are not criminals and
at the worst are merely victims of venial human frailties.
The lustful, the gluttonous, the avaricious and the prodigal,
and the wrathful are punished in a measure out of proportion
to their faults.   These weak people should not have been put
in hell at all.   They are not really wicked as most of the faults
they have are personal and do not inflict extreme pain upon
others.   Yet the poet parcels the unfortunates off to the
second, third, fourth and fifth circles respectively, and makes
them suffer severe agonies.   The carnal sinners shriek and
lament as they are smitten by hurricanes; the gluttonous howl
like dogs because of the hail and rain, as they lie on the ground,
the avaricious and prodigal with great howls roll weights by
the force of their chests and the wrathful are covered with
mud, striking and mangling one another piecemeal with their
teeth.   Yet all of us have the instincts of these sufferers and
we do not like to see our fellow creatures in such travail.   We
grow indignant at Dante because he devises punishments other
than those nature inflicts upon them for being in the grip of
such passions.   Is not dyspepsia sufficient punishment for the
glutton?   Is not poverty the natural sequence of prodigality?
Is not a debilitated physical condition the result of sensual
practices?   And does not anger nearly always make men
commit follies that they later regret?   We do not need any
other hell invented than that people find here.

The victims in the first and the sixth circles are no sinners
at all.   Those in Limbo, the first circle, happen to have had

the misfortune of having lived before Christ.   They may have
led exemplary lives, they may have made the greatest contri-
butions to human thought and left mankind many heritages,
but since they had never been baptized they sigh eternally.
Here are the great Greek philosophers and Roman poets.   It
matters little how noble were the deeds of many of the ancients,
it is of no avail how profound were their ideas; these people
must remain in hell since they did not subscribe to the theological inanities adopted by Dante.   Many of the Old Testament characters, however, escaped hell by a special favor of
God.   Dante has been severely criticized for his Limbo, and
the injustice of this creation is admitted.

In the sixth circle the poet places such an intellectual man as
Epicurus, because he held the soul mortal with the body.
Heretics are here, and this means that many of the best of the
world's thinkers lie here lamenting and baking in the red hot
tombs.   Of course the whole conception is distinctly medieval
and only those who believe that a liberal minded philosopher
is doomed to burn in hell while the insipid theologian will go
to heaven will derive pleasure in reading the canto describing
this circle.   Mention should be made that Dante puts here
the father of his intimate poet friend Guido Cavalcanti, and
hints that hell awaits the latter also.   But heresy is no longer
a crime; indeed it generally argues a mind freed from dogma
and superstition.

In the lower three circles where the violent, the fraudulent
and traitors are placed we have more horrible punishments.
When one recollects what terrible pain is caused temporarily
by a bruise or a burn, he will strongly condemn a poet who
invents excruciating physical tortures with which to punish

for eternity; he will rage at the delight that the poet takes
in witnessing the frightful calamities the victims suffer.

The only way to reduce the poet's whole scheme of punishments to an absurdity is merely to enumerate the punishments
in one of these lower circles of hell. Let us take the eighth
circle called Malebolge, or evil pouches, which is divided into
ten budgets. Here lie in all their misery those who practised
deceit or fraud of some kind. Descriptions of their horrible
agonies cover fourteen of the thirty-four cantos which comprise
the *Inferno*.

The panderers and seducers were going about naked, whipped
by horned demons and, naturally, under the circumstances,
were lifting their heels continually. False flatterers were
whining, puffing their nostrils for they were plunged in human
excrement, and the head of one was so foul that he was un-
recognizable. The simonists were plunged head downwards
with their feet and part of their legs extending upwards from
circular holes. Their soles were on fire and caused their
joints to twitch. The false prophets were walking silently
weeping, but their heads were stuck on their necks backwards,
so that their tears fell upon their hips. The barrators or
corrupt officials were boiling in a lake of pitch, and whenever
one showed himself, devils amused themselves by pronging
him. They drew up one victim and clawed and flayed him,
till he fell back again into the lake. In the sixth pouch were
hypocrites walking slowly weeping; they were hooded and their
eyes were covered by heavy leaden cloaks gilded on the outside. In the seventh pouch were horrible serpents among
which ran thieves whose hands were tied behind by snakes;
these fixed their tails and heads through the men's loins.
Serpents and men changed one into another. The reptiles

darted at the robbers, interwined with them and thus the
transformations went on constantly. The fraudulent coun-
sellors were enwrapped by flickering flames of fire. In the
next pouch were the sowers of discord and schism. Poor
Mahomet was cleft all the way down the belly with his bowels
hanging out; another man was cleft from chin to forelock and
as he walked around his wounds were closed up till a devil
opened them again with a sword. Another had his hands
chopped off and he smeared his face with blood. Still another
carried his own head in his hands by the hair as a lantern
and lifted it in the air and spoke from it. In the tenth pouch
were alchemists, false personators and other falsifiers. There
was a horrible stench here; two shades were leaning against
each other and scratching off each other's scabs.

Dante has however devised even more unique and cruel
punishments than these. Among the traitors in the ninth
circle we have Count Ugolino whose head was frozen to that
of an archbishop, which the Count was gnawing and devouring
at the nape. Then conceive Lucifer sticking half-way out of
the ice with three immense faces, black, yellowish-white and
red, weeping with six eyes, while tears and bloody drivel were
trickling over his three chins. Beneath each face came forth
two wings larger than a ship's sail, which the fiend was flap-
ping. In his mouth he chewed three other traitors.

To all this we might say *cui bono?* To heap horrors on
horrors, to conjure up such loathsome afflictions, to perpetrate
such fiendish barbarities is evidence of vindictiveness and
cruelty in the poet and we begin to hate him more than we do
the sinners. It is sad to contemplate that Dante even believed
in the reality of these punishments and that he invented them
for the next world by seeking them on earth. There is some-

thing rancorous, something malevolent on the part of one
to make a list of crimes and inflict upon those who practise
them such merciless tortures.   To an age which even seeks
to alleviate the pain of the temporarily imprisoned the malice
of a man who punished for eternity by torture is all the more
revolting.

Yet the admirers of Dante defend these punishments on the
ground that they are the logical retributions brought upon the
victims, not by Dante, but by the crimes themselves.   He is
supposed to make the penalty fit the crime.   The suffering is
said to be the fulfilment in the next world of what has begun
here; the hell depicted is alleged to be in man's own heart.

But where is the connection between the dripping bowels
of Mahomet and the fact that he founded a religion which
has millions of adherents but does not meet with the poet's
approval?   There is no ingenuity in punishing the man who
carried his head in his hand like a lantern, by separating his
brain from his trunk, because he once separated a father from
a son.   There is no reason for punishing traitors by ice because
of their coldness, any more than in making heretics subject
to fire in accordance with the medieval tradition.   The conse-
quence of robbery is not shown by making thieves steal the
bodies of serpents.   There is no relation between the corruption of barrators and the lakes of pitch into which they are
plunged.   The lesson that sin carries its own damnation with
it is not shown by depicting gluttons torn to pieces by a three-
headed dog, amidst falling hail.   And we must admit that
some sins like usury never carry any evil consequences for
the usurer, but should be avoided simply because an undue
advantage is taken of a fellow creature.   Other sins like defi-

ance of God are purely imaginary on the poet's part; one might as well defy the law of the conservation of energy.

It is also claimed in defense of the poet that his age needed revolting images to convey moral lessons and that he saw his own thoughts transformed into real though horrible pictures. But this will not extenuate the matter. For us such images offer little of any value. They arouse our smile often when meant to awaken our terror. This method of teaching a moral lesson is extinct and authors to-day give us more effective pictures of the evils caused by certain vices. The consequences of avarice, drunkenness, seduction and adultery have been shown more effectively in some of the novels of the nineteenth century than in Dante's poem. No one expects these vices and crimes to be extinguished by literature; and our modern writers are often greater artists because they are interested in studying the sinner and depicting his emotions than in pointing directly a moral, as Dante does. The fact that Dante used these revolting images renders him of less artistic value to us, nor should we forget that he believed in the reality of his images.

Dante has not succeeded in showing that a man is punished by that wherewith he sins. He has simply run the gamut of the most fiendish sufferings and distributed them among some sinners. He has deliberately searched for instruments inimical and deadly to the body and to life and has employed them upon poor wretches, chiefly Italians of his age. We hold our nostrils as we read; we cover up our ears; we hide our eyes. Did one ever before see brought together such stinking odors, filth, excrement, blood, mutilated bodies, agonizing shrieks, mythical monsters?

Dante punishes his sinners for one offence only, although most people are guilty of several sins. Thus there are traitors in the ninth circle who, having also committed murder, should be in the stream of boiling blood in the seventh circle. But it would be rather difficult to have a man in several circles of hell at the same time, so the poet picks out the worst crime and punishes him for that alone. There have been people who were guilty of almost all the sins and crimes that Dante mentions, though it is hardly likely that there were many who were free from a single one of the vices punished in hell. Had the poet known all the details of the lives of his saints in heaven, he would have found that most of them also could have been placed in some circle in the nether regions. Men cannot really be ticketed off and labelled with some sin; most folk have tendencies to several faults. Dante's whole scheme of punishment is unfair. Hypocrites and magicians, thieves and flatterers are punished more severely than murderers who are placed in a circle above them in hell. According to Dante usurers are more wicked than adulterers, magicians more deserving of chastisement than degenerate perverts. We have Cæsar among the virtuous heathen in the first circle, though we know he also belongs among the carnal sinners with Cleopatra. The poet is cruel to suicides who ought rather to be pitied; he is lenient to the contemptible Paris who stole another man's wife and caused a great war.

As a matter of fact we all belong simultaneously to the hell and the heaven of Dante. If I have the fault of being a glutton and am nevertheless a just man, should I be placed in the third circle of hell and no attention paid to the virtue which would entitle me to a place in heaven? Should not my noble quality of that rare virtue justice make the poet lenient to my venial fault of prodigality? There is not a man who is not guilty of some sin, there is not one who does

not possess some virtues.   Great deeds and a noble character
can wipe out the memory of certain sins; the commission
of some crimes can never atone for the possession of some
good attributes.   We may pardon a kind man his anger but
we will never forgive a murderer because he was a theologian or a fighter for the cross.   The final judgment to be
pronounced upon men should be made by weighing all their
good and evil qualities.   We often are content to see a man
with some faults provided some great virtues go therewith.

Then Dante does not think of studying his victims and
their sins.   He is too interested in railing at vices to pay
attention to them as objects of research.   He is always the
moralist, never the psychologist.   Unlike Spinoza, who studied
all the baser emotions disinterestedly, he could not analyze
the maladies of the soul without uttering the harshest rebukes.
He is like a physician who, called in to diagnose and cure a
disease, would spend his time in railing at the patient instead,
for becoming sick.

So Dante condemns everything and everybody, kings, poets,
popes, friends, statesmen and even mythical creatures of
antiquity.   He curses cities and piles the most vituperative
epithets upon them.   He tells Pistoia to decree to make ashes
of herself; he invites Florence to rejoice because her name is
spread in hell and says that if the calamities which her enemies
crave for her befell her it would not be too soon.   He hopes
the Arno River may drown every person in Pisa.   He refers
to the same river in his *Purgatorio* where he describes its
course through towns which are referred to as the dens of animals.   The river flows past the abodes of foul hogs, curs,
wolves and foxes by which are meant the cities of Casentino,

Arezzo, Florence and Pisa respectively. As for the Genoese, he asks why they are not scattered from the world.

One sees examples of his cruelty in the way he treats some of the unfortunates in hell. He asks Virgil to have the cruel Filippo Argenti soused in the broth of filth in the fifth circle, and when the wish is gratified he thanks God therefor. Virgil approves of Dante's attitude and himself says to the wretch, " away there with the other dog." Dante remarks on another occasion, when a serpent coils himself about the neck of a blaspheming thief, " from that time forth the serpents were my friends." But Dante's wrath exercises itself especially on two traitors. He pulls a tuft of hair out of the head of one of them in order to make him reveal his identity. This was the infamous traitor Bocca degli Abati, who was responsible for the defeat of the Guelphs of Florence. The other instance of the poet's reprehensible conduct is in his treatment of Friar Alberigo, who killed his own brother and nephew. This traitor begged the poet to lift his frozen eyelids so that he might weep a little and ease his woe. The poet promised to do so if the friar would tell his name. When Alberigo did so, Dante broke his promise, saying that to be churlish to him was courtesy.

Dante makes even Virgil brutal and has him quote from Aquinas some inhuman statements. When Dante wept at the sufferings of the soothsayers, Virgil tells him that he should pity no one in hell, that a man is a criminal who is moved by compassion at the judgments of God, no matter how cruel they are.

Most of the characters in hell however are Florentines and the poet revenged himself on his enemies by putting them here. He has been severely censured for sending his master

and teacher Brunetto Latini to the circle where degenerates
were punished.   Dante is bitter against the sin of ingratitude,
yet what worse ingratitude do we find than his conduct here?
He is aroused by sorrow, but he might have kept silent on the
score of his teacher's sin.   The episode is one of the finer ones
of the *Inferno* and is very touching.   If a man remembers
even his friends in his scheme of punishment we may expect
little mercy from him for his enemies.   And many of the
characters in hell are obscure people of whom history makes
no mention.   The folly of the poet's scheme may be seen if
we were to imagine some man in public life to-day placing
many of his contemporaries in hell.   Conceive of a poet con-
signing American presidents, poets, generals and statesmen to
the lower regions.

One of the artistic weaknesses of the *Inferno* is the intro-
duction of monsters and demons in hell, in some cases to take
part in the punishment of the victims.   Commentators find
allegoric significance in the poet's choice of mythical creatures,
but it is generally conceded that bad taste was displayed in
the choice.   We have Charon, who had about his eyes wheels
of flame, ferrying the damned souls across the Acheron;
Minos, the judge who girded himself with his tail as many
times as the grade he willed that the damned be sent down to
hell; Cerberus, with three heads, red eyes, a greasy black beard,
a big belly, barking and rending the gluttons.   We have the
hideous Furies with serpents for hair and the human-faced
Harpies with their feathered bellies.   There is the Minotaur
Bull and the serpent-bodied man-faced Ceryon.   Two of the
most preposterous conceptions of the poet are in his making
the Centaurs shoot with arrows at the murderers in the river
of blood, and in his account of the sport in which the demons

indulged by prodding the barrators in the boiling pitch. The last monster who appears is Lucifer himself and he is the victim of one of the punishments. His body is about fifteen hundred feet long and his haunches are surmounted by the poets who thus enter purgatory.

But fortunately there is some merit in the *Inferno* and this is due to a half dozen or more episodes. These show pathos, sorrow, tragedy of genuine human interest and possess artistic value. The most famous of them all is the sad story of Francesca da Rimini, a story that has been used by other poets as themes for drama and poems. Deserving almost equal fame is the celebrated tale by Count Ugolino of the starvation of his sons. The story moves us with more terror than the description of the punishments in the lowest circle where the tale is related. Dante had command of the art of making our flesh creep by relating a true tale; he did not need to contrive horrible tortures.

It is a pleasure to discover these little tales here and there and we will mention them. There is something pitiful about the suicide of Pier delle Vigne, a poet who killed himself because his eyes were put out; instead of seeking for more of his brief but sad tale, Dante and Virgil ask him to tell them whether the soul is ever loosed from the tree, into which every suicide has been changed. The meeting of Dante with Pope Nicholas III is fine, because of the irony in the exclamation of the simonist pope when he mistook the poet for the then living Pope Boniface who was expected here. We are moved by the description of his thirst which the counterfeiter Master Adam gives to his visitors; we read again with interest the story of his wanderings which that fraudulent counsellor Ulysses tells; we follow the story of Guido de Montefeltro as he relates how he told Pope Boniface not to keep a promise, though we lose the sense of reality in his tale when he tells how the Black Cherubim snatched him from St. Francis and carried him to hell. We note the poet's conversation with Farinata, in the circle of unbelievers, about the battles between the Ghibellines and the Guelphs, but the conversation relapses into frivolity when the poet persuades him to explain why the dead can foretell the future but are ignorant of the present.

Having seen Dante as a painter of the horrible, let us consider him as a religious thinker and a contemplator of ideal happiness. We shall examine his *Paradiso* which some critics regard as the most profound of the three divisions of his poem, although it has been the least popular. Much of the section is nothing more than theology in rhyme. We will take up the second section, the *Purgatorio,* last.

Dante divides his heaven into ten parts, since there are different orders of blessedness for no other reason than that it so pleases God. Seven of the heavens are named after the sun, the moon and the five planets then known. The last three are those of the fixed stars, the crystalline heaven and the empyrean. These abodes are inhabited by saints, theologians, crusaders, apostles and other religious folk. Only three of the regions are not inhabited by the specially religious. These are the heavens of Mercury, Venus and Jupiter which are the dwelling places of followers of fame, of lovers and of righteous kings respectively.

There are about ten cantos that treat of theology alone, while there are a half a dozen cantos that are unadorned biography and history. All this occupies about one-half of the *Paradiso* while the rest of the poem consists of accounts of the heavens and of the curious deeds of the spirits there. Let us examine the contents of some of these theological cantos; let us study some of the representative heavens, such as those of the sun and of Jupiter where the theologians and righteous kings respectively dwell; let us also traverse the highest heaven, the empyrean. We shall carefully go through the historical and biographical cantos, for Dante interests us most when he refers to this earth. We shall then see how much merit the *Paradiso* contains.

Dante plunges very early into his theological and historical discourses. At the conclusion of the very first canto, we have Beatrice's discourse on the ordaining of the universe by Providence. As is frequently the case with her, it is an explanation which does not elucidate. In the next canto she gives a curious account of the origin of the spots on the moon. She maintains that the diverse virtues of God acting through the Angelic Intelligence, shine through the moon diversely and hence create the distinction between light and darkness. In the third canto she shows that souls do not go to the stars, as Plato thought, but rather to the empyrean; she then proves to her own satisfaction that there is no injustice, that the very fact that God's justice seems unjust to mortal eyes is argument or proof of faith. She also sets forth the doctrine that people who have good intentions when forced by violence of others to break them must nevertheless not receive credit for their virtue; that they should be punished for a wrong they committed through no fault of their own. The viciousness of Beatrice's arguments does not interest us so much as the poet's approval. He says that her speech so overflows him that he can scarcely thank her sufficiently, and that the intellect is only satisfied when it is illumed by the truth as in the present instance. Then the poet wants to know if man can make

satisfaction for broken vows. She explains that a vow may
be changed with clerical dispensation if the matter substi-
tuted exceeds in worth that of the original vow. Then follows
a canto of history, the story of the growth of the Roman
Empire, told by Justinian in the planet. Mercury; next we
have Beatrice's arid discourse on redemption and then the
talk by Charles Martel in the planet Venus on the impossibility
of imperfection in the universe and on the cause of variety and
diversity everywhere.

Thus the reader has traversed eight cantos of the *Paradiso*
and the only bit of poetry that he has encountered is the brief
story of Piccarda Donati telling how she was forced to leave
the cloister and thus break her vow. Even her narrative is
ruined by theological dogmas when she explains why spirits
in the lower division of heaven cannot envy those in the higher
ones; she concludes with that overrated line " His will is our
peace."

When Justinian tells the history of Rome he does so to
illustrate the poet's belief that the Roman Empire existed
by Divine Right because Christ was born and died to save
mankind during the supremacy of the Empire. It was by
the authority of Rome that Christ died and saved man; all
this was especially ordained by God. God made Rome the
mistress of the world so as to save us all. The only reason
that God made Rome go through its period of history was it
should reach the times of Tiberius and of Titus, as in the
reign of the former Christ was crucified and in the reign of
the latter this crucifixion was avenged upon the Jews in the
destruction of their temple. God was happy at both events,
he ordained and waited for the death of His son and yet He
punished the Jews for causing it; and He made the Roman

Empire prosper so as to bring all this about.   When Justinian
is not advancing this most amazing and ludicrous theory he
gives us dry history.

But Justinian's historical tale becomes the text for an
elaborate and hopeless discourse by Beatrice on redemption.
The substance of it was of great importance to the poet and
for that matter still is to many people.   She explains to the
poet why God wanted and expected the Jews to crucify Jesus.
It was because Adam's original disobedience was so great that
no amount of human humility could atone for it, so God Himself had to take the burden on his shoulders.   Adam's sin
was atoned for by Christ's death; God's son himself had to
die for it.   Man was created directly from God and hence
needed a God to die for him.   Another futile discourse of
Beatrice is the one about the creation and the nature of
angels.   We learn that the angels are pure form, that they
are infinite, that no two are of the same species, etc.   She
even appeals to the authority of Jerome and then denounces
teachers who do not agree with her absurd views.   She attacks
traffic in indulgences though not indulgences themselves.

Nor should mention be omitted of the examination to which
the poet was subjected by three of the saints in faith, hope
and charity.   The poet's views of faith are worthy of com-
ment.   Faith according to the poet is belief in something
that cannot be proved; it is supported by its own substance
and hence is called evidence also.   The proof of faith that we
have is the Bible which is divinely inspired.   The miracles
prove that the Holy Writ is true, even though we know of
them through it.   But because the conversion of the world
to Christianity without miracles would have been a greater
miracle than any in the Scriptures, the Bible must be true.

After this convincing and irrefutable argument the poet tells us that his faith is belief in a God and in the three eternal persons who are of one essence. The picture of St. Peter examining the poet and appearing as one of the flaming spheres upon fixed poles and revolving as within the fittings of clocks and then encircling the poet thrice because he was so well pleased with the answers is undignified.

There can be very little doubt that among the most ludicrous portions of the poem is the heaven of the sun, where the theologians were. The poet commences with a discourse on astrology; he becomes confused, as does also the reader, and he then throws aside his task, saying, " Henceforth feed thyself." The authors of theological books are made to perform amusing feats not in keeping with the seriousness of their calling on earth. They wheel around the poet and Beatrice thrice in the form of shining lights. Thomas Aquinas names them and they wheel around again singing and keeping time. They cease and revolve again. Meanwhile an inner circle of lights, who are the spirits of some other obscure theologians enter upon their gyrations, matching motion with motion, song with song. They danced, exalted and sang together. The effect was as if one ring of brilliant stars revolved around another. They sang not of Bacchus and Pæan but of three in one. They would occasionally cease, to give St. Thomas or some one else an opportunity to talk.

These theologians were all authors of books full of false speculation, which are unread to-day. For some reason or other Solomon is one of the theologians, although because of his amorousness and idolatry he should have been in hell.

Thomas Aquinas is the first spokesman and he enters upon the following important problem. Why is Solomon not as

wise as Adam and Jesus, since he has the reputation of being
the wisest of men? The reason is he was not created immediately of God as they were. St. Thomas then goes into some
unintelligible and meaningless details about creation; and
concludes that after all Solomon was only the wisest king.
He is somewhat confused by his own explanation, grows angry
and attacks some authors who did not agree with his views,
and comments on the vanity of human judgment. The next
equally important problem that is to be solved is the following: When the resurrection comes how will the eyes of the
resurrected bear so strong a light as that in which the spirits
are now clothed? The spirits dance and rejoice that the
question was raised. It was so intricate and difficult that
they asked Solomon to answer it. Solomon answers that at
the resurrection the body will receive new glory and our
power of vision will increase. An amen greets the solution,
and the spirits even show a desire to have their bodies back.
These are examples of futile medieval problems that the poet
seriously entertained. It must be understood also that he
gave full faith to these explanations.

What a hopelessly clouded brain Dante had! When the
great pioneers of the Renaissance were teaching the people
liberal views he was trying to make them penetrate deeper
into darkness. He ignored the heritages of the times; he
turned away from their splendors and set to verse notions
that were vapid and paltry. He hated original writers, and
was the great foe of individualism. He bowed abjectly before
authority.

In the heaven of the sun the lives of St. Francis and St.
Dominic are recited. St. Thomas tells of St. Francis's poverty, dwells on some details of his life and describes his alle-

gorical marriage to the Lady Poverty. The narrative concludes with an outburst against ecclesiastical abuses. The life of St. Dominic is narrated by another saint who tells of his exploits, of his wedding to faith and of his smiting heretical stocks with most vigor where the resistance was greatest; the tale ends with an attack on the backsliders in religion. Both of these biographies might have been contributed to a dictionary; they are really space fillers here. The characters do not interest us, at least as examples to emulate, though all the world has loved St. Francis.

It should be added that in the various declamations against the church and popes and religious practises, the poet simply rails at some surface abuses. It never occurs to him to question the whole structure of the supernatural or the very foundations of institutions; he never probes deeply. He points out flaws here and there but he does not apply the scalpel to the putrescence beneath.

The conception of the heaven of Jupiter, the abode of the righteous kings, is probably more risible than that of the dwelling place of the theologians. All the spirits here including King David know Latin. Some of them shaped themselves into letters of the alphabet, forming a brilliantly lit sentence in Roman letters. They formed, while flying and singing, the words from the Book of Proverbs " Diligite justitiam qui judicatis terram," " Love righteousness ye that be judge of the earth." At the last letter M the lights spread out into the head and neck of an eagle, who is a symbol of monarchy and hence, according to the poet, of justice. The eagle sang and explained to him that Divine Justice is beyond our comprehension and should be taken on faith.

The eye of the eagle is King David; and the eyebrow consists of five lights, also earthly kings, two of whom are pagans, Trajan and Rhipeus the Trojan. The Roman king is in heaven because he became alive again after being in hell and then believed in Christ, according to the legend, while Rhipeus believed in redemption, through God's special grace.

The eagle next presents to itself for solution a plausible argument against Divine Justice. Where is the justice that condemns a man who was born a thousand miles away and never heard of Christ, through no fault of his own? Why should he not be saved if he has lived a righteous life? After calling those who ask such questions, earthly animals and gross minds, the eagle gives an answer which amounts to this: So much is just as is consonant with the Primal Will which is the Supreme Good. Then the bird names some unjust kings and calls them by vile epithets.

As we see this eagle of brilliant lights we can scarcely resist picturing to ourselves a bird formed of electric lights such as we see in advertisements, lighting up whenever the reading matter, also of incandescent lights, goes out in darkness. No one will be led to practise justice by seeing this awkwardly conceived eagle. Most certainly the poet regards any speculation as to the existence of Divine Justice as a great heresy. But as a matter of fact there is no justice in nature, where all living animals feed on one another, where suffering and pain are common, where might and chicanery usually triumph. Justice has no connection with religion but is a convenient arrangement to prevent misery among men. It springs from a moral sense in man just as hatred of ugliness arises from an æsthetic sense. It evolved with other sentiments such as pity and fear, in the natural evolution of man from his savage state. The conception of justice shows the general moral view-point held by a community and changes with time and place. To nature, our conception of right means nothing; she takes no interest in the fact that we may follow worthy human ideals and yet suffer therefor. A savage has notions of justice also; one could no more expect nature to pay tribute to them than to our own.

Many who are willing to concede that there is little if no literary merit in any of the parts of the *Paradiso* so far referred to, find it however in two other sections, first in those cantos containing the story, declamation and prophecy of Dante's ancestor Cacciaguida whom the poet meets in Mars among the fighters for the cross and secondly in the concluding cantos of the poem where the empyrean is described.

Of the episode about Dante's ancestor, it may be said that it contains those oft quoted lines prophesying the poet's exile, lines which do linger in the reader's memory: "Thou shalt make proof how the bread of others savors of salt, and how hard a path is the descending and mounting of another's stairs. And that which will weigh heaviest upon thy shoulders will be the evil and senseless company which thou wilt fall into in this valley." There is an impassioned paragraph where the old soldier contrasts the luxury of the new Florence with the simplicity of the old, and we like his parting advice to Dante to attack severely. But there are too many obscure names and too much genealogy and history which have only local significance. The crusader is of no interest to any one and we know of him only through Dante; he is here because of the poet's vanity. Except for a few passages, the episode about the poet's ancestry is out of place in the *Paradiso*.

But the poet's admirers have adulated the account of the empyrean. The chief attribute of this region is the flood of dazzling light that exists here; the poet lays so much stress upon this that our eyes become blinded and we want a little darkness. There is the river of light in which the saints are mirrored. It becomes a vast rose, wherein are descending thousands of angels like a swarm of bees, their faces bathed in flame, their wings in gold and their forms whiter than snow. Beatrice soon takes a place along with Virgin Mary and some of the women mentioned in the Bible, such as Rachel and Sarah. There are places for saints and innocent children; there are various degrees of innocence for no other reason than that God so wills it. The poet through prayer of St. Bernard to Virgin Mary obtains grace, and soon sees God Himself and the poem ends. He makes again and again famous addresses to light but he is really calling darkness. Every one reading the poem wonders that the insignificant Beatrice and the women of the Old Testament who had no particular virtue, should be in the rose in the highest heaven while Aristotle is in hell.

No one wants to be in this rose, if this is the highest goal for the human race. This place is not for heroes or thinkers or benefactors to humanity. The poet has brought together puerile conceptions that do not appeal to us. His Beatrice is indeed theology. As an ideal of women she is absolutely extinct. One cannot help speculating whether she has any passions at all. She is bloodless, characterless and unreal. She was an ideal to the poet and we sympathize more with his account of her in his *Vita Nuova,* for there she appears to be a live woman. But here she irritates and repels us.

She drives the poet into an abyss of falsehood instead of leading him to knowledge.

Let us now return to the second section of the poem.

Dante's Purgatory is a mountain that arose from the waters in the southern hemisphere, in antipodes to Jerusalem and was forced out by a portion of the earth which fled when Satan fell. The top of this mountain is the earthly paradise, while the slope is divided into seven ledges for the purification of sinners.

The earthly paradise is described in the last cantos of the *Purgatorio*. There is a lengthy description here of the procession of the chariot representing the church. This is drawn by a griffon, half eagle and half lion, who symbolises Christ. Beatrice sits on the left hand border of the chariot. The griffon ties his car to the mystic tree which was at first barren and now blossoms forth. Then an eagle descends upon the chariot, which is also attacked by a dragon, and we see seven heads with horns, and a harlot and giant kissing each other; finally the giant drags the wagon off into the woods. The eagle is representative of sins of the empire, the dragon carrying off part of the car represents a schism in the church, the seven horned heads are the deadly sins, the harlot and giant are the pope and the king of France. There are other symbols; there are twenty-four elders representing the books of the Old Testament, and winged creatures behind them who stand for the four evangelists; there are ladies typifying the virtues. We find little to move us in his account of the procession; moreover Dante imitates the Apocalypse too closely.

The first meeting of the poet with Beatrice displeases the reader. She rebukes him for having paid attention formerly to other women, and whether the reference is to Dante's amorous affairs or to his backsliding from theology, she annoys us with her jealousy and intolerance. We also have her prophecy about the mysterious DXV, 515, who will save the country. Then there is an account of the geography of the earthly paradise, of the origin of the winds here and of the sources of the two streams Lethe and Eunoe.

Let us now examine the region called ante-purgatory and then some of the ledges of purgatory proper.

There are pictures and scenes in his *Purgatorio* that are among the best Dante wrote, though they are few, but the underlying idea of purgatory is as pernicious and absurd as most of his other ideas. The application of his theory of repentance produces strange effects. A great criminal repents on his death-bed or acknowledges regrets for his crime and he is consigned to purgatory, which means that he will ultimately reach heaven. A venial sinner like some wrathful or gluttonous men, may be accidentally killed or die suddenly and have had no opportunity to repent and he becomes a suffering denizen of hell for eternity.

It is easy to repent, but that does not undo the consequences of our sin. Most murderers regret their deeds after killing but that does not restore life to the victim, or assuage the agonies of the relatives and friends. Those who maim, ravish, betray can usually make no reparation for the wrongs done and hence their repentance is of little avail. Nor does a man's disposition usually become changed by repentance. Place him in the same situation and he will generally do the same deeds again.

In ante-purgatory are the souls of those who died in the contumacy of the church, the negligent who postponed repentance to the last hour, spirits who delayed repentance and met

with death by violence but died repentant, and princes who
had been negligent of salvation. These must wait various
periods of time before they can get into purgatory proper;
these periods of time may be shortened by the prayers of the
good on earth. A mere accident might have prevented repentance and the repentants might have been in hell. The negligent who postponed repentance to the last hour, might have
been suddenly killed and thus their chances of salvation would
have been lost. Then the doctrine that the prayers of good
people will shorten the periods of suffering in ante-purgatory
and purgatory proper is indefensible.

The punishments of these who repented of the seven deadly
sins are also cruel though not as much so as those in hell.
The proud were going under their load, more or less burdened
and weary; the envious were covered with coarse hair-cloth,
and iron wires pierced their eyelids; the wrathful wandered
about in dense smoke; the slothful were running and crying
out examples of diligence; the avaricious were weeping, lying
on the earth turned downwards; the gluttons were compelled
to gaze at fine apple trees whose fruit they could not pluck,
and hence were hollow-eyed, pallid, and wasted; while the
lustful spirits moved in flames of fire. The repentant sinners
were all compelled to recite verses and were shown examples
of those who practised different conduct from their own. As
the poet ascended the ledges each of the seven p's which an
angel had traced on his forehead dropped off.

There are also scientific and theological discourses in the
Purgatorio, though not as numerous as those in the *Paradiso.*
We have the lengthy discourse of the poet Statius in the seventh
ledge, on generation, on the infusion of the soul in the body
and his explanation as to why the spirits of the gluttons are

lean; there are discourses by Marco Lombardo on free-will
and the corruption of the world, and by Virgil on the classifi-
cation of the sins and on free-will. Statius's account of the
trembling of the mountain which is due to the rising of a pure
soul to heaven is another one of the risible follies that crowd
Dante's poem.

Nevertheless the *Purgatorio* contains more human scenes
and finer pictures than either of the other two portions of the
poem. It is better literature and has several episodes that
deserve to be permanently read for their beauty. It also contains the poet's famous impassioned invective against Italy.
There is the celebrated picture of historical figures who were
guilty of pride, and of their punishment. The poet makes
the passage effective by his vivid impressionistic touches. We
again see Niobe in tears, Saul upon his sword, and Troy in
ashes. There are also examples taken from history of humility
engraven in the rock. We again see David dancing before the
ark, and Trajan promising to help the widow avenge her slain
son. We also like the conversation between the poet and
Oderisi of Gubio, a votary of the art of illumination. The
description of the ledge of pride is quite successful, even
though diatribes in literature against the deadly sins are
obsolete.

We are also interested in listening to Casella singing a
canzone of Dante at the latter's request; we admire the account
of the meeting of Statius with Virgil and the fine tribute paid
to him. We rejoice in the meeting of other poets like Sordello
and Guinicelli with the author of the Æneid. The memory
of his wife Nella which moves Forese Donati stirs us and we
revel in his attack on the Florentine women.

But a poem must be judged as a whole, and the central idea behind it; the philosophy to be gathered from it must be considered. As a poem with a purpose, the *Divine Comedy* is a failure not only because of its inability of conviction, but because of its perverted view-point and its emphasis on the trivial. The poet seeks to make us more moral chiefly through theology. Besides being free from sin and crime, we must, according to his view, subscribe to the belief in the trinity, in original sin, in the atonement, in the miracles of the Bible and in the divine right of the pope. We must be baptized, we must not have the slightest doubt of the efficacy and power of prayer, we must say mass, we must not question belief in resurrection. Satan must be a real creature to us. The saints must be regarded as still working miracles; the angels must be actual denizens of the skies in whom we must believe.

The poem makes re-echo in our ears those words repeated in all religious books for the last two thousand years—" sin," " repentance," " beatification." In fact these words sum up the whole intent of the poem. We must be conscious of our sins, we must repent of them and thus attain beatification. Dante wishes to make us be bowed down more heavily by the burden of our sins; he persuades us to search them out; he wants us to be united with God, which really means to be attached to the dogma of a creed. He slanders human nature most foully and seeks to impose upon us imaginary obligations for its redemption.

The idea of sin, like a worm, eats through the core of the poem and makes it unpalatable. And many a thing is sin according to Dante which is sometimes trivial, and sometimes actually meritorious. To differ with authority, to follow out your own destiny, to set at naught superstition, to defy unsound institutions, are sins according to the poet. He is harsh in condemning if he sees that you possess all those human instincts which you are justified in cultivating; he rails at traits of the flesh which it is natural to be inherent in it; he maintains all faults should be exterminated but he does not understand that if such were the case many of our virtues would go along with them. He is ever setting up before us the conception of sin as the only reality in the world; he sets horrible examples before us; he finds a panacea for it in the worship of dogma.

The poet endeavors to show us how we may reach the highest form of life; he has a definite theory as to its nature. But no one would seriously recommend to us to-day the scheme that the poet has in mind. We do not want pictures of the sufferings of the worst criminals to serve as examples to us not to commit like crimes. Why rail against the crimes of murder, robbery, treason? Who asserts that they are not wrong? It seems that when the poet is in the right he is always commonplace. Why also set before us the ideals of men who never spent time in reflecting rationally on matters of earthly and human importance, but instead on monstrous and fabulous problems, on the solution of absolutely futile and inane questions? If Dante had at least tried to show us the beauty of a life devoted to important study and noble elevation of spirit and relief of one's fellow creatures; if he had conjured before us images of figures who sought to develop their own abilities, who sought not after too much theology, who were not afraid of daring speculation, we would have hearkened to him.

He cannot forget his scholastic philosophy; he loves theology more than art. It will be noticed that he is always greatest where he is least dogmatic; he is inevitably inartistic and sterile when his theories absorb him. Many of the characters he meets spoil their tales by giving expression to a tenet of Aquinas. They are often mere mouthpieces for the solution of some petty question that puzzles the poet. He is the defender of almost every idea against whose truth thinkers and writers of merit fought before and after him. He would have placed in hell and excluded from heaven, almost every really great man of artistic power and intellectual attainments who has ever lived. He judges rather than studies, he asserts rather than explains.

He troubles us with political questions that have long lost their value. We to-day do not find any interest in the theories that divided the Guelphs and the Ghibellines, except from a historical point of view. We do not care about the strife between the pope and emperor, about the theory whether the emperor holds directly from God as the Ghibellines and Dante with them maintained. We believe that no one gets his power by divine right. The poet's political views are introduced often and form the basis of many of his judgments. Though we cannot expect him to give even a passing thought to the theory of democracy, the fact is that the political theories in the poem help in making much of it as obsolete as does the theological intent.

Again there is entirely too much local history in the *Divine Comedy* to give it universal significance. The dissensions, the contemporary and petty affairs that figure constantly, detract from the emotional appeal of the poem. The endless obscure names of the catalogues of murders must be read with a history of the times in hand. Unfortunately most of Dante's historical narration is not lit up with the profound reflections or picturesqueness such as we find in some of the great histories of the world's literature. A poem that seeks for permanence should rise above the discords of the poet's town and should be free from partisanship and prejudice.

The critics of Dante are usually of two kinds. Those who come to him for intellectual nourishment are generally those who are antagonistic to free thought. They have been, it may be added, the best students of the poet and have interpreted him best, because they have found much that is still true for them in the comedy. They naturally find their own souls mirrored here and one cannot quarrel with them for their admiration. One should first dispute with them the truth of the theories they maintain. But there are other critics who accept none of Dante's ideas but look upon him as a painter and poet who has an excellent command of the language and a magical power of expression. They see the greatness of the epic in the fine similes and brief descriptions both of which in most cases take up a few lines. But can we look upon Dante as a world poet for this alone? Many writers of our day are finer literary artists than he. As a matter of fact many novelists who have no universal significance have surpassed him in descriptive powers. Æsthetic critics of Dante forget that it was not his similes and descriptions that first brought the poet fame, that it was his theories and ideas which were first regarded as his real distinction.

Countless essays and books have been written on questions raised by the poem that have no value or importance. If some one could but make a list of the problems aroused by Dante we would have an excellent example of the useless learning often wasted on classics. But we wish our poem to be both of æsthetic and intellectual value and not a means of studying mythology, geography, pseudo-science, theology and history. The commentators have written essays and books to decide whether Beatrice was a real woman or only represented theology, whether her rebuke to Dante was for his heresy or immorality; whether she foretold the coming of Luther, whether she was married or not. They have speculated on the question whether the allegory was political, religious or moral in its intent; they have fought about the extent of the poet's Catholicism and have even found him very liberal. They have been divided as to whether there was an analogy between the scheme of the purifications of the seven sins in purgatory and the punishment of the crimes and sins in the nine circles of hell. The poet's minor allegories and his fabulous creatures have all been given significance.

There is not a single character who is a hero because he championed advanced ideas. There is not the slightest reference to the conflicts which man has with institutions that harm him; nay, these institutions are held up before us as beacon lights. There is not a passage that considers from a broad view-point any of the problems of man's relation to the universe at large. Expression is not given to the emotions that we all know, in our voyage through life. The poet does not dwell on the sadness of man's position in the hands of destiny, or the calamities brought about by poverty or ignorance. He is an enemy to freedom, to toleration. He has not shown us any sympathy with an individualist.

The poet was behind his own times. He had courage in condemning abuses, but after all he attacked flagrantly apparent misdeeds. He assailed a few kings and popes, but popery and monarchy were ideal institutions to him. He sided with the majority in all matters. He did not quaff from the fountain of which all the great intellectual leaders of the Renaissance drank; the few ancient authors whom he read had no broadening effect upon him; he read his own religion into them. Can any one imagine the pagan Virgil speaking thus like a theologian. " Mad is he who hopes that our reason can traverse the infinite way which One Substance in Three Persons holds. Be content, O human race, with the *quia* (i. e., with the existence of a thing rather than the cause of its existence) ; for if you had been able to see everything, there had been no need for Mary to bear child." Virgil is supposed to represent reason, but he is made the mouthpiece of the most unreasonable statements. Never has a poet been more distorted and perverted by a disciple than has poor Virgil at the hands of Dante. It is really not Virgil who is speaking but Aquinas himself; it just pleases the Italian to call the speaker by the name of Virgil.

Had there been no other writers of the poet's time who had escaped from the bondage of asceticism and dogma, from the belief in revelation and the supernatural, we might not censure him and would attribute his errors to his times. But those times were a period in which these ideas were losing the great sway that they wielded in other ages. And Dante was not one of the elect who held up before humanity higher ideals. He might have been pardoned for having written his poem a few centuries earlier, but not for having sent out such a product of superstition at the dawning of an enlightened age.

One of the leading defects of Dante as a thinker and hence as a judge in moral matters is his uncompromising and undeviating adherence to the doctrine of free will. He has not the slightest doubt as to the power of man to control every move of his body, every inclination of his soul, every tendency of his

mind, every humor of his temperament. He does not see the
slightest virtue in the theory of determinism which shows that
man often is but a puppet for whom the wires have already
been pulled to play his part here. He does not consider that
often we are the victims of heredity, of environment, of circumstances. A Jean Valjean would have repelled him. He
believes that man has been made evil by his rulers, by the fact
that the pope and emperor did not govern independently in
spiritual and temporal affairs respectively. Hence the poet
can give us no plausible views on the subject of good and evil;
he does not measure them by the amount of pain they bring;
he does not derive them wholly from the presence of the moral
sense in man; he does not weigh them properly in connection
with the rest of the universe or show that they are but human
conceptions. We therefore can expect very little sympathy
for a wrong-doer from Dante; we only find it in cases where he
knew personally some of the sufferers. He does not divide the
goats from the sheep; all sinners of one species are hustled
together; if he ever excepts some one it is because some one
prayed for him.

Dante sums up the leading ideas of the medieval ages in his
poem. As a compendium of ethics, religion and philosophy
of the popular kind which prevailed in the dark times before
the Renaissance, it may merit study by those interested. As
a living poem most of it is hopeless. All we find in it are a
few episodes that might have been written independently. We
are not concerned about what is going on in his heaven or hell,
but are interested in the speeches of some characters who
related what went on in this world. If the poet could but
come back to life and see that we discard the so-called truths
that he taught and that we linger over some of the tales colored

by emotion, he no doubt would think we were laying stress on the secondary portions of the poem.   He would probably claim that these stories were incidental or illustrative, but were not the *raison d'être* of the poem.

What a spectacle of a poet trying to give us the last word on human wisdom, and we allow our childish fancy to revel in some idle tales in the poem!   What an ironical situation it is when we dismiss the passages meant to save our souls and pay most attention to a story of adultery in the poem!   Behold Dante striving to win us to heaven, and we instead ponder on his exile, his anger, his sorrow.   As a moralist who would redeem us we find him useless and instead we find enjoyment in those passages barren of ideas, but telling of simple events like the meeting of one poet with another.   It is a strange fate that some poets undergo and yet very justly so.   Can one conceive of Dante's indignation on discovering a fine critic like John Addington Symonds ignoring the weighty philosophical discourses and explanations of the universe in the poem and waxing enthusiastic over a simile?   If a poet would teach, and gives us the poorest intellectual product of the time, this is the fate he deserves.   Great ideas that remain true for ages, couched in artistic style and lit up with emotion, will not suffer the fate that much of Dante's poem has experienced.

When the reader of the future thinks of Dante's poem it may be as a medieval literary product in which have been imbedded several literary jewels like the stories of Francesca, Count Ugolino, the Apostrophe to Italy, the account of the examples of pride sculptured on the rock and of humility engraven on the pavement in the first ledge of purgatory, the prophecy of Cacciaguida and probably another half dozen episodes.   These will be all that is left of the poem.   A very small residuum, the reader will say for a poet rated so high. But Dante has left some other poems and a few passages of excellent prose, though also an obsolete political treatise. His figure with the hatchet face and sharp features weighed in grief, wandering about in exile and refusing to return to his native city under humiliating conditions will always live. As a type and personality of his time he will interest us. As a world poet his position ought to decline. But a poet he will essentially remain.

MILTON: PARADISE LOST

Paradise Lost holds the distinction of being the greatest narrative poem in the English language. It is a tale of the origin and history of all of man's misfortunes; it also attempts a solution of them. It treats of the creation of the universe, of the justice of God, of the origin of evil; it offers an explanation of the theory of free will. Its leading characters are supernatural or mythical beings in whose existence the poet believed; its scenes of action range throughout the entire universe. There are descriptions of battles between devils and angels, which of course never took place; there is the tale of how Paradise, the garden of Eden, was lost, although it never existed; there is the mournful event of how human nature lost its perfection, which it certainly never possessed.

Let us examine the poem and see how much of it remains vital, poetic and profound to-day. Let us note what effect the growth of advanced ideas in science and philosophy has made upon our critical judgment of it as a work of art. We know that most of the axiomatic ideas in the sphere of thought to-day are just the reverse of the views that Milton entertained. The chief difficulty that we find with the poem is that it is built upon a theological system that is false and upon a demonology that is monstrous. We shall discover that the poem is vitiated by the presence of the Ptolemaic system of astromony, which the poet deliberately chose for his purpose though he knew the Copernican system was the true one; we shall be irritated by intricate studies of supernatural creatures; we shall be wearied with pedantic and bookish learning; we shall be in the mazes of infelicitous secondary allegories;

above all we shall learn that the central ideas of the poem are fabrications unworthy of being the foundations of a literary performance. Yet we shall find a sublimity and majesty of style, and an excellently drawn portrait of Satan. We shall read beautiful descriptions, find our intellects and emotions stirred by a few speeches; and shall note great narrative powers displayed here and there.

Critics always warn us that in reading the poem we should for the time being forget that we are in the midst of mythology, and that we should suppose the story to be true. But we cannot resist the promptings of our feelings. Our sense of truth is offended; we find the absurdities too palpable; all laws of probability are defied; the inconsistencies are too numerous. We become bewildered by the mythological machinery. We cannot follow Lucifer in his peregrinations throughout the universe. We are confused by the dividing up of heaven and hell and cannot conceive of the events taking place therein which the poet describes. We inevitably find ourselves subjecting the fiends to the laws of nature, and painfully struggle with our imaginations in making ourselves believe that they can subsist in vacuity. We who wish to know more of human events on our planet cannot stir up interest in supernatural events in chaos. We also cannot forget that the poet simply commentated upon the first few chapters of the Bible; that he took seriously some legends whose truth no one would seriously defend to-day and which were disregarded by thinkers even in ancient times. He spoils the tales by adding a tissue of irrelevent foreign matter read into them by theologians, such as the story of the devil entering the serpent, the battle of God with Lucifer who is trying to take revenge on God, and the sin of Adam demanding atonement by the death of God's son.

The most famous books of the poem are the first two. Here there is little or no theology; here we are not yet troubled with those two inconceivable individuals, Adam and Eve. We have the picture of a defeated general, even though the poet does call him Lucifer. Many critics regard these two books of the poem as the only ones in it deserving of enduring fame. The secret of their greatness is in the speeches scattered through them. Milton who intended to justify the ways of God towards man and show us the cause of all our woes, is remembered for some speeches of his devils which are good because of their wordly wisdom. No doubt even these speeches have been overestimated, and the frequency with which they have been quoted has made them somewhat commonplace. But they are real literature and time has not as yet made them obsolete. The very first speech of Satan makes us admire his dauntlessness, his noble arrogance, his determination never to yield. We think of him as of a defeated human being and forget that his battle is supposed to have taken place with God; we retain in our memories those words about the unconquerable will not being lost. Then we feel sorry for him when he contrasts hell with the place he had lost. And we have his well-known reflection about a mind being able to make a heaven of hell and a hell of heaven; and his policy "better to reign in hell, than serve in heaven." There are about seven speeches in each of these opening two books and most of their contents brim over with expedient, non-moral, Machiavellian plans. The spirits seek a goal and will allow nothing to hinder them. When they resolve, as the archangel advises them, on war "open or understood," and to work by fraud what force cannot effect, somehow or other we are not repelled by the insidiousness of the scheme planned.

The speeches in the second book might have been spoken at a gathering of defeated chiefs who are deliberating whether to continue the war, sue for peace, or retreat altogether. We have the passions of revenge and hatred shown in these monologues and the character of each rebel angel shows itself. These devils have fine intellects, and utter thoughts naturally suggested by the circumstances. We admire them all, Moloch with his vindictive nature, and Belial with his common sense about the futility of further resistance in the face of the impossible. We are even more impressed by the suggestion of Mammon to make the best of the present situation and get accustomed to it. As a matter of fact every speaker is convincing. When we finish these speeches and turn to the other portions of the two books the contrast is great.

We have the pedantic and absurd descriptions which make us remember that the rebel angels are not human, though we were being led to believe so from the human reasoning in the speeches. No, we do not care for the picture where Satan and his crew lie in hell. The place is not real, the tortures never occurred, everything is incongruous. We are not impressed by the picture of Satan chained to the burning lake. All the pedantic comparisons which the image of the archfiend arouses in the poet's mind are ludicrous and have been unfairly admired. We have the simile about the Leviathan who is often mistaken for an island, whom Satan resembles. There is the description of Satan's shield, which is compared to the moon and then Galileo's name is drawn in because he had perfected the telescope. What would we to-day think of a poet who used the sun in a simile and then brought in the name of Kirchoff because he had invented the spectroscope? The host of Satan reminds the poet of autumn leaves in

Vallambrosa, then of the reeds on the coast of the Dead Sea, the name of which evokes the story of Pharaoh and the Children of Israel. As the angels rise and fly the density of the swarm is brought home to us by reference to Moses's locusts, and the number of the spirits is suggested to us by mention of the invasions of Rome by the Goths, Huns and Vandals. The army of the angels was such as to put to shame the largest forces in the annals of the world; even all the knights who jested at Aspramont and Montalbron, and elsewhere were mere pygmies compared to them.

Milton reaches the climax of pedantry and inartistic writing when, imitating Homer, he gives us a catalogue of the names of the leaders of the host. By some strange metamorphosis these angels are the very heathen gods whom later the nations in and about Palestine worshipped. Every god is tagged and described by his various surnames; the extent of his earthly jurisdiction is also given. The counts in the bills of indictment consist of the leading crimes of which he was guilty later in the course of his earthly career. This little band whose whole combined realms occupied a very small piece of land, defied the Creator of the universe.

There is too much of the school-room in Milton's poem. He is always being reminded that such and such an event in hell bears a resemblance to some historical event that took place later on this earth. He displays his scientific knowledge, his information in mythology, his theological studies. When he describes the rising of Pandemonium, the palace where the angels are to sit in counsel, he does it with his usual pedantry.

But the poet also moralizes and badly, in these two opening books. There is the immoral assertion that tells us God allowed Satan to proceed to commit crimes in order that he might heap up damnation for himself. We are warned not to be surprised that riches grow in hell, for that soil may best deserve that precious bane.

While Satan is going to explore this world and try to lure man from the right path, as this was what the spirits had decided to do in order to be revenged upon the Almighty, the other angels amuse themselves in his absence. The whole picture is ludicrous; they are supposed to be suffering with fire and yet they can sit there and discuss freewill and providence, or play the harp; some compete in racing, others for amusement tear up hills and rocks or go out exploring hell. Milton knew his Homer and he reproduces scenes here from the Greek poet's mythology. The chief thing that can be said in extenuation of this whole scene is that we are at least saved the torturing scenes we find in Dante. No character in hell, human or diabolic could think of amusement in playing a harp.

The lengthy allegory of the birth of death through Satan's sexual relations with sin, and then of the incestuous relation of death with the latter, its own mother, is repulsive. The account of the hell-hounds begotten by death creeping into the womb of their mother sin is nauseating. The story is unconvincing and seeks to show us that sin brought death into the world, and that Satan was originally responsible. However one wonders why sin is made by God to be the portress at the gate, when He knew that she would give Satan the key.

We have pointed out some of the merits and faults of the two first books of the poem. Thus far in spite of some good speeches and the sublime style here and there it does not appear that the poem ought to rank very high. As yet little of Milton the religious thinker and sensuous poet has appeared. We shall have him in these two rôles in other parts of the poem. We shall find more Miltonian descriptions and more pedantry and puerility. But we have seen him in his highest role, the creator of the character of Lucifer, who has some dignified traits.

The other book of the poem that ranks high with many critics is the ninth. Here we really have the story of the temptation of Adam and Eve, their succumbing thereto and their downfall; the action and substance of the poem.

We cannot immediately resist thinking that a poet who teaches that the eating of an apple was the cause of the greatest misery that ever afflicted humanity has chosen a wretched and trite theme for a great poem. The story is too trivial to us to penetrate into the allegory behind it. Yet from the start the poet is impressed with the greatness of his theme which he tells us he thinks much more heroic than the idea of revenge that prompted Achilles to fight on account of the death of his friend.

The arguments between Adam and Eve who wishes to work alone in another part of the garden are commonplace. Adam cannot persuade her to remain by his side even though he discourses about free will. Then Satan disguised as a serpent finds her and is almost moved not to prosecute his aim by the sight of her beauty. He flatters her and uses fraud. He pretends that he is able to speak because he had eaten of the tree of knowledge. He explains to her that she will not die by eating of the forbidden fruit; he ate and lived to tell the tale. Eve eats and immediately her intellectual powers grow. Where before she was in absolute ignorance she now possesses

supreme wisdom. We cannot appreciate this sudden change
in her. We have never been in her situation; our own knowledge is a matter of gradual growth and we have not been
placed in a condition wherein from almost total insensibility
we sprang instantly into the possession of a great intellect.
It would be as if an infant suddenly became a philosopher.
So she is not undergoing a transformation that we have ever
experienced.

The entire dialogue between Satan and Eve has been entirely
over-praised. Eve's arguments reek with silliness. She does
not give any reason for refusing to eat except that she was
forbidden to do so; she believes that she will die for no reason
but because she had eaten. After Eve makes Adam eat, fear-
ing that in case she died he would wed another Eve who does
not even appear on the horizon, they both begin to have all the
passions natural to human beings, shame, remorse, suspicion,
anger, mistrust, hate and love. We do not find ourselves
depicted here, for we were never without feeling or the capacity
for passion and then discovered them suddenly in ourselves.
It is as if two statues had suddenly come to life. We cannot
sympathise with people who suddenly received all the human
faculties, for we have never been without these. Whatever
instincts and emotions we possess have evolved in the growth
of the human race; no one has received them suddenly.

At first Adam and Eve could not distinguish between good
and evil but after having eating the apple they can do so.
How they receive this power we are not told any more than
why they were forbidden to acquire it. There is no reason
given why they should not have eaten the fruit. But why
have the tree growing in the garden where they may always
succumb to temptation? The final impression that Milton

unwittingly gives us is that God Himself is responsible for their calamities. If He made man without strength of will, and knew that he would not exercise his will power, why did He let man decide his own fatal destiny?

When we read a story of temptation and fall, trailing dire disaster, we have the right to expect that these calamities will be the natural consequences of succumbing. A person may seek inordinate fame or illegal love, or ill-gotten wealth and hence lay in store for himself griefs that he might have naturally anticipated from his quest, but we cannot perceive how eating an apple will bring about all the disasters of mankind. No allegorical interpretation can save the situation.

The rest of the poem is, with the exception of a few additional speeches and descriptions obsolete. In fact there are many sections that are notorious as illustrating the low level occasionally reached by a sublime poet. There are whole books that are scarcely redeemed by any virtues whatsoever. They abound in antiquated science, astronomy, theology. They set forth conceptions borrowed from mythology, they paraphrase chapters of the Bible, they invariably mistake falsehood for truth, ugliness for beauty. They incorporate Milton's political and religious views, now no longer tenable. Scarcely any topic of human interest is touched upon.

For instance four successive books of the poem, the fifth to the eighth inclusive, may be dismissed almost *in toto*. They are occupied by conversations between Adam and the angel Raphael who tells him of the war in heaven between God and the rebel angels, and Christ's victory over them; then the creation of the world in six days is described. The angel had been advised by God to go down and tell Adam about the plot of Satan. Raphael's account of the physiology of angels and of their digestive process is about as preposterous as Adam's philosophical explanation to Eve of the cause of dreams.

We also hear from Raphael how God begot a son to whom all the angels had to bow. One finds the son out of place here in heaven before the time when he was to go down in the world to preach his sermon on the mount. There is no mention of him in the opening chapters of the Bible, although theologians and commentators have read his name into these sections as they have done also in the love poem called " The Song of Songs " and other parts of the Old Testament. We are not interested in knowing why he was created after instead of before the angels, although we would like to know why God delegated many tasks to His son, such as sending him out to rout the rebel angels. The son is described as riding on a chariot, convoyed by cherubim with four faces and bodies set with eyes. Fires flashed, smoke belched, ten thousand saints followed. The son had a bow and arrow to cast lightning, and his ensign blazed. Later the son helps create the universe for God, having circumscribed it with a golden compass. We found the same son in the third book discussing theology with God, and we must confess we are not overwhelmed by his heroism when he offers to die for man. He is a colorless character. Milton failed here completely for the son bears resemblance neither to a human being nor a god; he is not subject to passion, yet he is not free from the possibility of death.

The reader is always wondering why God allowed the rebel angels to rebel, since He is omnipotent. Still we find that He even suggests that He might lose Heaven; and He also displays lack of dignity in the derisive attitude he maintains towards Satan. We continue to wade through the story which the angel Raphael is telling to Adam. He shows us how the angel Abdiel refused to join the rebellious forces, combating Satan with commonplace arguments and rebukes. Satan replies in a speech showing his usual intellectual powers.

The story of the war in heaven occupies the sixth book. Naturally most of it is reminiscent of the wars of Cromwell. The bringing of cannon into heaven has always been the subject of much ridicule. The conception of angels and devils fighting like human beings is in itself ludicrous, but it is made infinitely more so by the use of military engines borrowed from man. Michael and Gabriel are sent out to lead the armies of God. Abdiel indulges in some preliminary ranting and thinks that he defeats Satan by words. The battle now rages and Satan and Michael meet in combat; the former is wounded and howls with pain, but the wound heals up for angels can only die by being annihilated; they cannot be mortally wounded. Satan invented the cannons after his first day's defeat, and the angels are temporarily thrown into confusion, but soon they tear up mountains and hills which they throw at the devils. The mountain throwing scene is usually passed over by Miltonians out of charity for their bard. It is at this stage that the son comes to the rescue. He drives the devils out of heaven with his thundering. He did not seek to annihilate them but to root them out of heaven and drive them into hell. But why should he not have exterminated them and saved the human race all its troubles, and also thus kept himself from dying for it? Why didn't the Almighty make the rebel angels respect His son before compelling the latter to defeat them? Why did the battle have to last three days and why didn't God Himself fight? Above all how did the narrating angel get hold of a copy of some of the world's epic poems to assist him in describing these wars?

After telling of the wars, Raphael describes how the world was created in seven days. He uses the language of the first chapter of the Bible and adds to and embellishes it. He is also quite an astronomer, but everything he says on this theme is out of date for us, because we know it is all neither science nor literature. We are aware that the theories of modern geology and evolution were not known in those days and we do not quarrel with Milton for his hopeless science, even though some of the Greek philosophers knew more about the subject than he did.

The story of Adam's creation as he tells it to the angel does not move us. We do not comprehend a situation where a man is born in the adult stage with all his faculties upon him and immediately gets an instantaneous impression of the novelty of the scenes before him. We cannot appreciate his feelings when for the first time he finds himself confronted with life. We ourselves get the impress of earthly things gradually by a long process. We have judged the world with the imagination of a child and the vision of a boy and the reflection of a man. We do not recall our first complete sight of the universe; we have never burst out into the full contemplation of life the instant after we had been in oblivion.

Then the whole scene where Adam suggests to God that he wants a wife is ridiculous. Imagine God joking and telling Adam that He has no wife, although we know He has a son; imagine the Supreme Being acting like a teasing papa who is asked by his child for a toy. The poet's sense of humor was not highly developed. But God admits that Adam is right, the animals were created with mates, why not he? So the creation of the woman from Adam's rib takes place and the first love affair in the world is begun. The angel hearing

Adam's story attacks the ravages of passion but adds that angels also love. We look in vain for a description of the feelings displayed by lovers when they first meet. There is nothing in the situation that has any human interest, because we have not met our Eves in this way. The whole story of the creation of man and woman and the universe is anything but literature.

There are two famous conceptions in the poem that have become well known through the sheer folly that Milton displayed in creating them, that of the Fool's Paradise in the third book and of the bridge built by sin and death connecting earth and hell, in the tenth book. The first region contains Catholics, seekers of fame and some philosophers and giants. The bridge built by sin and death over which Satan sends the two engineers down to the earth is a direct result of the eating of the apple. God sees sin and death take possession of the earth and gives a very poor reason for allowing them to do so. But he does so because he wishes that the filth caused by man's sin may be licked up and that the son may have an opportunity of flinging both of the malefactors out of the earth. However the angels sing that God's decrees are just, although we wonder why He did not interfere and save the world so much pain and spare His son's dying to save man. We also cannot help smiling at Milton's implicit belief that great calamities have afflicted the world because of Adam's sin. The seasons changed, the winds blew so that spring should not smile perpetually, the animals began to devour one another; all because of the eating of the apple. None of these catastrophes ever took place before, according to the poet. We cannot enter into the spirit of the allegory simply because we know there never was any connection between any deed of man and the changes in seasons or butchery of one another among animals; for these events took place long before man came.

There is nothing more cruel in the poem than the kaleidoscope of future calamities that is shown to Adam and Eve by the Angel Michael. Adam faces the horror of seeing all the troubles of the world that he has caused. The consolation that he gets is that the son will set everything right. The image of death is shown to him so vividly that there can be no possibility of his forgetting it. He sees one of his own sons kill the other, who rolls in the dust and blood. Moreover the generous angel shows Adam a lazar-house where he sees all the afflictions that are to kill his children, madness, epilepsy, ulcers, colic, atrophy. Then he is forced to utter a real reasonable and rebellious sentiment. Why is life given to him to be taken away thus? Who would not refuse to accept life or give it up if he knew what was to face him?

No doubt one of the most effective sections of the whole poem is the last third of the tenth book where we have Adam's lament for his fate, and his quarrel and reconciliation with Eve. For once they become actual human beings with passions and despair. Adam's lament is rich in intellectual display and emotion. We have the unhappy blind poet speaking here. We forget that the lament is about something that never happened; we imagine now that the punishment is real. Why did God create us and then allow us to suffer? Why were terms made with us in the formation of which we had no share, and in the keeping of which we find ourselves hampered? The rebuke to Eve is very likely taken from the poet's own household, and we are interested in Adam's anti-feminism. But soon we see the finer side of his nature after he hears her pathetic lament, in which she is the mouthpiece of womankind. Eve's suggestion of suicide is not entertained by Adam and we are happy to know that they can derive consolation from the fact that they will be able to wreak revenge on the serpent. One regrets that so much art and passion should have been wasted on an imaginary sorrow. But nevertheless here Adam is ourselves, and his fears and cries are our own.

There are several other powerful scenes in the poem, especially Satan's address to the sun, and we might add the description of the Garden of Eden. The latter may suffer somewhat because of too many mythological allusions, but we find it altogether a good piece of landscape painting. The address to the sun might have been spoken by Napoleon at St. Helena.

But there is so much in the poem that makes it antiquated and dull. The Lucifer whom we admired in the first two books loses his interest for us. We are amused at the idea of his lodging in the sun and of his changing into various animals like a toad, a cormorant, a serpent. We yawningly observe him escaping Gabriel's watch, only marvelling at the stupid angel with shield and helmet, unable to do his duty. A messenger must glide down a sunbeam to warn him. We look on almost contemptuously at the scene where Satan in the form of a toad is speared by the angel's messenger to be made to assume his real shape. Satan's debate with Gabriel bores us, and we are amused at the poet's conception of God hanging up a pair of scales, which show that Satan will be defeated in his combat with Gabriel. We rail at the criminal negligence of the angel in deliberately allowing Satan to escape, but this had to be done to help Milton's scheme. And God is presumed to be looking on and does not hinder the arch-angel's escape. When Lucifer accomplishes his mission and returns to tell the other devils of his success we are not frightened when they turn into horrible serpents and attempt to eat of the fruit of the tree which turns into ashes in their mouths. No, we merely say to ourselves, that the poet can become very grotesque.

Thus we might continue pointing out dead matter in the poem. The dialogues in Heaven between God and the son, occupying the first half of the third book are examples of God as schoolmaster in theology. Then there is Adam's explanation to Eve that the stars shine at night because total darkness might regain the world and extinguish all living things, and also because millions of spiritual creatures walk the earth unseen and need the light. Nor do we care to have from a writer who gave us some excellent tracts in defence of divorce for incompatibility of temperament the commonplace apology for the wedded love of the pair, and the address to matrimony. And we are not impressed with the story of her creation which Eve narrates to Adam and which is overheard by the serpent. Nor does the account of her falling in love with Adam move us. She had never seen nor heard of a man before and hence had no passion, so we do not feel there is any merit in her story of the birth of love in her soul. No woman ever found herself suddenly created and suddenly facing a man. No man ever courted a woman as Adam did Eve.

That Milton took this apple eating seriously is proved by a prose work of his which was discovered about a century ago. In the volume he says that eating the apple was the greatest crime because it was a transgression of the whole law. It included ingratitude, disobedience, gluttony, parricide, theft, sacrilege, deceit, lust, irreligiousness, pride, etc. Adam committed all these crimes when he ate the apple. The poet says that some particular act in itself indifferent had to be forbidden to test man. But some deed in itself wrong and carrying within itself the seeds of its destructive powers would have served better as a theme for a poet. If Adam had been forbidden to commit a crime and he was disobedient, we would have been able to appreciate the consequences of his conduct and the poem would have carried a stronger lesson.

The poet never succeeded in proving his main theme. God knew beforehand that Adam was going to eat the fruit of the tree, and hence be the cause of sin and death. Yet He allowed him to do so, and did not hinder him and the poet thinks he has justified the ways of God to man because God made man's will free. It was man's fault if he could not exercise his will-power. But God might have made man's will stronger; it would not have involved any additional difficulty for Him. God sees the greatest evil impending and instead of averting it, allows the most frightful calamity to pursue man. Why did not God undo Satan's work immediately? He should have done more than merely send the angel Raphael to warn Adam. He should not have permitted the watchman angel to allow Satan to gain an entrance to this world. He should not have allowed Adam and Eve to separate for thus Eve fell a prey to the wily serpent. The poet has not succeeded in showing God's justice; he attempts to defend it only by futile theological discourses.

Nor does the poet show us God's goodness, which consists in allowing His only begotten son to die for us. First, history has shown that calamities have harassed even those who followed closely in the son's footsteps, that great religious wars, massacres, persecutions, have troubled those who accepted the son. Secondly, since many horrors spread over the earth before the son came, why did he wait thousands of years and not

save man sooner? Why, besides, should God show Himself
such a poor father as to allow His son to die, even though the
latter gladly offered himself up.   Thirdly, many of us believe
that the death of no one can save the entire race.   And then
there are people who believe that this son of God was simply
a human being, the son of a carpenter, and that his real virtue
is that he tried to spread a pure though unpractical morality
among men.   No, we do not find God's goodness in the poem,
when we see that after all Satan triumphed; he accomplished
his end; he brought about his object to ruin humanity, he
brought death and sin into the world; in short he worked
revenge on God and is the victor.   He has never been put out
of commission and has continued to work evil down to this day.
The only thing that God did was to promise redemption by
the death of the savior.   But Lucifer accomplished far more
evil than the good that was to be brought by God's son.   Milton's God was a miserable bungler; he lost out on the whole
and must resort to apologies and promises.

The moral views to be extracted from the poem amount to
the trite advice not to be disobedient, even when you are not
given a reason for submission.   Milton who fought against
authority and defended the murderer of a king, who championed the liberty of the unlicensed press and the liberation
of the marriage ties, in this poem is the defender of authority,
the enemy of freedom.   The poet was himself a rebel who sang
the praises of subordination.   But no definite lessons are
really taught us; we simply understand that the poet means
we should spurn Satan and follow Christ; or avoid evil and
pursue virtue; and this is really vague, for he does not show
a profound perception into the nature of either.

He offers us no consolation but repentance. He is not impressed by any other duty in life, but the expiation of sin. He attacks ambition; while Dante at least placed the ambitious in heaven, Milton puts them in the Fool's Paradise; yet he himself was ambitious. He does not speak highly of love or woman in the poem; we know that he thought of his own domestic misfortunes when he drew Eve.

Professor George E. Woodberry has pointed out a radical defect in *Paradise Lost,* namely that there is a denial of progress in it; the idea of the poem is one of restoration to a former state than that of revolution. The epic becomes one of the " damnation of things, in which the fact of final partial restoration is present as an intention and promise only. There is what makes it a poem of past time, and removes it far from the modern mind." And this is true. There is really no hope but an angel's promise. Everybody's deed affects some one who is innocent. Just because Satan rebelled, Adam had to suffer; because Adam sinned death came into the world; because Eve ate the apple Adam fell; because the race suffers Christ was to die. Yet there is so much talk of free will and we see that each brought consequences against which the will was unable to combat. We never want to go back to a former state of civilization; we seek to have something different and in accordance with our new environment. We would not have the early state in which Adam and Eve found themselves before Satan came, even if we could. We try to adjust ourselves to altering circumstances and are contented if we find little struggle in doing so. Development, progress and evolution are subjects not touched upon in the poem.

Milton's borrowings and lack of originality have been pointed out by critics and commentators. The theme he chose had been handled by contemporary poets whose works we know- he had read. He borrowed plots and passages and imitated other poems rather freely. Students have compiled quite a list of poems from which Milton derived copiously. We know that he was certainly influenced by the *Lucifer* of Vondel the Dutch poet. Milton also plucked plumes from the poets of Greece, Rome and Italy. He is particularly indebted to Homer. He recurs to him again and again; he eagerly appropriates similes, episodes and descriptions from the Father of Poetry. Yet he derives most from the Bible, in some instances reproducing passages almost word for word and line for line. He also incorporates arguments from books of theology and draws on scientific works for some of his astronomical data. If we were to consider only the original portions of his poem, by abstracting the borrowings we should have a production far less bulky than the present form. But it must be admitted that few could adorn what they used as Milton did.

We are all interested in Milton's personality. We know the stern champion of English liberty; we sympathise with him in his pathetic blindness. We are affected by his domestic misfortunes and his disillusionments as a husband and a father. We admire his resoluteness and his devotion to his ideals. But we must not let alien considerations influence us in determining his position as a poet. The time is even now at hand when all that remains of his work as a poet are some passages from *Paradise Lost* and a few of his minor poems. But what will most likely happen is that his prose works will be sifted by critics and we shall have many pages of impassioned prose in which he appears not as a theologian but as a clear and bold thinker. In no work of his does he rise so high as he does in his four treatises where he main-

tains opinions on the subject of divorce, which even our
own time finds too radical. In the *Doctrine and Discipline
of Divorce* and in the three pamphlets which followed, he
wrote from his own experience; he tried to support his
ideas by quoting too freely from the Bible, but he gave
sufficient proof to establish his contention that incompatible
temperament and contrariety of mind should be grounds for
divorce. He, the Puritan, is so modern in his views that he
shocks the liberal mind of to-day. There seems to have been
a conspiracy of silence among critics to ignore these books of
Milton, because they do not countenance the conventional
views of society. Yet the time may come when passages from
his divorce tracts will be on the lips of all thinking men while
most of the *Paradise Lost* may be forgotten. Books dealing
with so universal a subject, offering a rational solution of
problems that affect many people are certainly of greater
utility and even artistic importance than a poem which depicts
situations that never existed and gives a false interpretation
of useless questions.

Milton's fate as a poet bears a certain analogy to that of
Dante. *Paradise Lost* achieved its fame because people
thought it contained a true interpretation of the nature of
justice, of the origin of evil, of the moral order or disorder
on this earth. It was presumed to have embodied an unshak-
able system of theology, an irreproachable scheme of divine
government, and now that the whole fabric has crumbled, we
admire the poem because of its grand style. The pious contemplated with admiration a work which in their opinion
summed up the ablest views of life, and to-day people speak
highly only of the style and rhythm. Milton who was looked
upon by many as a divine seer who penetrated behind the veil

of the mysteries of life is remembered now for his skill in ornamenting the English language. He himself had contempt for the lyricists of his time who turned felicitous phrases; yet we like him, as does Matthew Arnold, for his " unfailing level of style." He is rich in lines of great beauty and power. We rhapsodise over his sublime passages, we are elated with his majestic sweep. He is expressive and many of his phrases are used by us daily.

But mastery of style is not enough to give one a place among the greatest poets. A world poet's production must appeal to us by the universality and truth of the underlying theme; it must be of great human interest and lack triviality. It should stir our emotions to the very depths, it should seethe with penetrating thoughts. There should be in it an " alliance to great ends " as Pater puts it.

On the continent Milton never won an exalted position. Byron has always held a higher place than he. There are several English poets however who have left us finer and more enduring poetry than Milton. He unfortunately attached himself to dogmas that have since been exploded and the ravages made by them in his palace of art have been too great and have shaken his position as one of the world's major singers.

BUNYAN: PILGRIM'S PROGRESS

Pilgrim's Progress has been praised for many reasons. First, Christian in his wanderings through many dangers, trials and temptations to reach the Celestial City is presumed to be a type of mankind in search of truth and righteousness. The allegory has won admiration because of the vivid pictures of scenes where Christian's hardest difficulties took place, such as of the Slough of Despond, the Valley of Humiliation where he fought with Appolyon, the Valley of the Shadow of Death and Vanity Fair. It has pleased because of the accounts of the pleasant stages in his journey such as the Interpreter's House, the Palace Beautiful, Beulah Land and the Celestial City itself. It is a work wherein are portrayed characters familiar to us all. Some of these are Pliable, Worldly-Wiseman, Mr. By-Ends and Great-Heart. Then the narrative has also charmed by its simplicity of style. We shall visit some of the places through which Christian traveled and talk with some of the people he met. We shall also extract the lesson taught by the allegory, and shall see what significance if any, Christian has for us.

Let us first examine the dangerous places through which Christian passed. We come to the slough of Despond, but *we* do not fall into it for it is made up of the doubts and fears afflicting repentant sinners. Only those who have upon their backs the burdens of sins against religion stumble here. We do not find ourselves obsessed by the horrible thought that we must be saved by following out the mandates of a church; we are satisfied if we do our duty to ourselves and our fellow men, and if we sin, we are willing to take the consequences in the natural evils that may follow us for our derelictions.   Christian's burden is not upon our backs and we do not sink into the ditch.   Besides it is not the most difficult thing in the world to refrain from crime and sin.   Bunyan wants to show us that to do good is so difficult that we must labor with an effort in that direction, and that we must be conscious of sin continually.

So when we find Christian soon engages in the struggle with Appolyon who is covered with scales, wings and is belching fire and smoke, we say to ourselves: " Now we have never fought this monster.   He is the same old dragon who is a constant figure in medieval literature."   We cannot understand why the dragon should be symbolic of sin against which Christian is struggling.   We are not even in suspense that Christian may be killed.   We observe with indifference, and incredulity that though his strength is spent he picks up his sword and drives Appolyon away.   Nor is there any vividness in the description of the fight, such as we find in the *Faery Queen*.   All that the poet tells us is that the dragon roared and that it was the " dreadfulest sight " he ever saw.

To us the allegory of good conquering evil, or religion fighting sin by means of a story of a man vanquishing a monster is no longer tenable.   It does not impress us, it is not beautiful. We are not overwhelmed by Christian's arguments with the dragon, and his reasons for leading a good life are not satisfying.   We do not feel encouraged when Christian tells Appolyon that God refuses to help us in order to try us out to see if we will not cleave to Him.   Moreover we do expect deliverance in the present world instead of waiting for the judgment day.   We have so many more effective examples in literature of struggles between good and evil that we do not have to recur to the dragon of our childhood days. We have wonderful analyses by writers of struggles within their souls and we don't need these conflicts visualized in this form.

We find the next terrible place through which we have to pass with Christian is the Valley of the Shadow of Death. We find here the same fires, howlings, ditches, chains, hobgoblins, snakes, mires, that we find in accounts of hell by other writers. Thus Bunyan means to show us the horrible side of sin, and the inference is that we must pass by all of these if we want to lead a virtuous and religious life. To us the whole thing is repulsive and unconvincing. We are willing to look at the Valley and forget about the allegory, but we cannot say that real horror is shown here. We think of more powerful descriptions we have read, of earthquakes, volcanic eruptions, dark forests, caves and shipwrecks, besides which Bunyan's horrors pale into insignificance. We never were in a valley of this kind and we walk through it unharmed and believe that all these horrors here must be products of Christian's diseased imagination.

The next obstruction in Christian's way is Vanity Fair. But he shuns everything in the fair that pertains to this world. He is averse to all forms of pleasure and to material possessions. He shows us that he will avoid pursuits that men usually follow. What a splendid opportunity the author had of giving us a vivid realistic description of the fairs as they existed in his day. His sole object in describing Vanity Fair was to point out to us that the eternal life is more important than the pleasures here. In this part of the allegory we have the ascetic author trying to rebuke us because we seek pleasures which it is natural for us to pursue; we go

with Christian here but we linger and shout at him not to
hasten, that the city for which he is bound is not any more
picturesque or alive than this place. Bunyan has unjustly
peopled his Vanity Fair with innocent tradesmen following
their natural calling in the company of scoundrels and gam-
blers. But we find that the chief commodity sold here is the
ware of Rome and her merchandise. So the fair was really
described in order to attack Roman Catholicism.

The redeeming feature of this portion of the story is the
account of the trial of Faithful and Christian for having
created a disturbance.

The sufferings of Christian and Hopeful in the dungeon
of Doubting Castle belonging to the Giant Despair are deline-
ated to warn us away from doubt in the supernatural and the
dogmas of the church. The lesson is that if we become sceptics
Despair will urge us also to commit suicide. We should,
like Christian, escape by using the key of Promise. But we
find that we can very comfortably put up in this castle and make
our abode here and not follow Christian any longer. We do
more than doubt; we know that Christian is wrong in his
views; we smile at him for having taken the journey; we may
as well tell him he is pursuing phantoms and that there is
only one Celestial City and that it is in the midst of the
so-called City of Destruction. We cannot depend on a man
who fears investigations by the intellect which are symbolized
by this castle. We also are annoyed at the conception which
gives Despair a wife Diffidence with whom he holds counsel
in bed.

After we have seen some of the terrible places and experiences encountered by Christian, we conclude that *we* have
never been through them. We may have found it difficult

to overcome temptation and obstacles, but we feel that after all these valleys and castles are not symbolic of our troubles. We shall look into some of the more pleasant places in the journeys and see if we have ever been in any of them.

The Interpreter's House was introduced to illustrate some theological lessons. There is the picture of the man looking upward, his back towards the world, to show Christian "that slighting and despising the things that are present" he is sure to have glory in the next world for his reward. The picture of the dusty parlor being sprinkled is supposed to represent the gospel cleansing original sin. The two children Passion and Patience are well contrasted but the story of the unfortunate professor who was locked up in the Iron Cage for eternity because he loved the pleasure of the world and did not follow religious edicts is insufferably poor in conception. The poor wretch was even denied repentance by God. And those of us who do not have Bunyan's fanatical ideas and do not shun life are also apparently to be confined. The description of the dream of the arrived judgment day is vivid and powerful, but fortunately we do not have such fancies. We are happy to escape such nightmares as witnessing the opening of the bottomless pit out of which issued smoke and coals of fire. The best scene in the Interpreter's House is the eulogy of courage as shown in the man who breaks into the palace.

When the burden falls off Christian's back at the sight of the cross we know that Christian is seeking a life not moral so much as religious. He seeks not righteousness but obedience to the doctrines of Puritanism; he is not permeated with a spirit of love and interest towards his fellow men, but he wishes to make them believe in the supernatural.

We observe that in the Palace of the Beautiful, Discretion takes care of Christian. Here the pilgrim sees and talks with Piety, Charity and Prudence. He offers a very poor explanation to Charity for deserting his wife and children. He also sees weapons that slew the wicked such as David's sling and the jawbone used by Samson. In the Delectable Mountains Christian was shown the broken pieces of those who were made to err " concerning the faith of the resurrection of the body " and lay unburied as an example to others. Christian also saw blind men walking about the tombs, victims of the Giant Despair; he inspected a byway into hell filled with brimstone, and would-be pilgrims who became traitors. He is too much entertained by seeing the poor wretches who were dashed into pieces because they did not subscribe to the belief in resurrection.

The description of Beulah Land and the entrance to the Celestial City has always won praise, but even here there is lacking such descriptive powers as we find in the great French Romanticists. We have the stock in trade objects wherewith ancient writers depicted heaven in order to make converts. There are the streets paved with gold, the ringing bells, the sounding harps and the angels, the trumpeters and so on. When Christian and his companion Hopeful cross the river wherein they leave their mortal garments, they are reclothed and then the Shining Ones describe to them the life of bliss that henceforth they will lead. They will wear crowns of gold and always see the Holy One; Him they will praise with shouting and thanksgiving; they will hear His voice, sit with Him when he passes judgment, and partake in the work of damnation. One sees immediately that the author's idea of God is idolatrous and that this God will allow all who are good Puritans to sit on the bench with Him.

Most of us have not been in these various places that were visited by Christian, nor would want to enter the Celestial City described. The ideal sought for is unworthy because the author seeks to make us reach it by inculcating in us the most fanatical theological doctrines. He depicts to us a goal which does not impress us as worthy of attainment.

Let us now observe some of the people whom Christian meets on the way. One will note that the characters whom Bunyan would persuade us are the erring ones happen to be the only persons who speak with wisdom. Those whom he presents to us for our condemnation meet with our approval. His heroes bore us, and insult our intelligence. The worldly types argue well and are more convincing than Christian. The author thinks that Christian is the victor in the debates, but he always is in the wrong. The real sensible and human types in the book are those who do not reach the Celestial City. These characters do not worry about salvation and the judgment day, and are live men like ourselves, and we take an entirely different view-point of them from what the author takes.

We cannot help admiring Obstinate for not being misguided by Christian and we command Pliable for returning home after sinking in the Slough of Despond. He argues well. Why should he trouble himself with the pains of a journey the nature of which he has already perceived? The struggle might be worth while if one is reasonably certain that there may be some results, but all that Pliable gets are promises. The Worldly-Wiseman is very discerning and reproaches Christian justly for meddling with. things too high for him. Christian does not heed his advice to go to the House of Legality in the Village of Morality, because it is too dangerous to reach on account of a hill; nevertheless men must have laws and moral codes which when founded on liberality of mind and charity of heart, can assist them greatly.

Talkative is well drawn. But he does not speak as sensibly as the author imagined he did. Bunyan quarrels with him because he does not practise what he preaches, and not because of what he says. But we feel that Talkative is too steeped in error and approve of his not living the life that he considers the right one. We are not displeased at Talkative's insincerity. May all those who think that they ought to pursue will-o'-the-wisps thus refrain from doing so! But nevertheless we have a good portrayal of a religious hypocrite, and though he does not utter as many absurdities as Faithful, he remains to us a type of the man who talks one way, but acts in another.

By-Ends is admirable for his shrewdness and good common sense. His characterization of the Pilgrims strikes one as true. They are intolerant and believe that a man must agree with them in every detail. Then they are foolishly on their journey in all weathers and they want to accomplish everything immediately. But By-Ends waits for wind and tide, takes all advantages in making his life secure; he thinks of his safety and scorns martyrdom. The characters Christian meets are wiser than he: he ignores good suggestions and practical advice. For instance, why should he not have heeded Demas's advice and have digged a little in the silver mine and thus have provided himself for life? One wonders how Christian subsisted on his journey. There is never a word about his desire for food, change of clothing, he does not have to earn a livelihood, he is troubled by no human wants; he never has any desire for such diversions as books, art or sport. He is not of this earth and we feel relieved when he reaches his haven.

The dogmatic way in which Christian and Hopeful argue with Ignorance is amusing. They flaunt before him such vagaries that we sympathise with him. It is refreshing not to be versed in all the errors in which they implicitly believe. They try to make him feel that he runs a possibility of damnation.

The heroes like Evangelist, Faithful, Hopeful and Christian himself are lifeless, without passions or rational thoughts. They tend to become abstractions, shadowy creatures to illustrate some Biblical texts. They are not moved by the ordinary things in life, they have not human failings. They walk blinded in their own conceit and ignorance, hoping hopes forever vain, believing things that will never transpire, seeking goals that do not exist. Their discourses are but words; they are frenzied in their imagination, hopeless in their reasoning, fanatical and intolerant. They do not so much attack abuses in morality as man's refusal to subscribe to their own pernicious religious notions. One feels about them as Atheist does: "I laugh to see what ignorant persons you are, to take upon you so tedious a journey and you are like to have nothing but your travel for your pains."

The book is really a series of sermons illustrated by allegory and symbolical characters. At times we have dry discourses themselves unillumined by metaphor. That we get many curious explanations of various matters is a foregone conclusion. The central idea running through the book is that of the conviction of sin in which we have all been born; the corollary is that we must strive for salvation so as not to be consigned to hell on the judgment day. Bunyan has recorded in his spiritual autobiography *Grace Abounding,* a pathological document in many respects more interesting than his famous allegory, how he came to regard ringing bells, dancing and reading romances as wrong. As a matter of fact to Bunyan every material desire smacks of sin. If we are reposing in the delusion that we are not so sinful after all, he seeks to remind us that we are. He seems to love sin, he thinks of it all the time, and hunts it out as with a keen sense of odor for it. He goes so far as to say that we can have right thoughts of God only when we think that He " can see sin in us when and where we can see none in ourselves," and that even when we have done our best and stand before Him in all confidence, our righteousness stinks in His nostrils.

Had Bunyan never possessed this deep conviction of sin, the *Pilgrim's Progress* would never have been written. Those of us who do not groan about sins that we have never committed and who do not look upon our human weaknesses as odious crimes, feel that the author has not narrated the history of our souls. Moreover we do not wish to be like him; we desire neither his mind nor his temperament. We do not wish to make much ado because the noble in us triumphs over the ignoble; we should not imagine we are so saturated with vice that to be righteous is a great task. A crimnal trying to reform or one suffering from religiomania may appreciate the allegory better than the average respectable cultured citizen.

No consolation is ever given. When Evangelist addresses Christian and Faithful before they enter Vanity Fair he tells them that one of them will die there an unnatural death, but that the deceased will be the happier one even though his pain is great " not only because he will be arrived at the Celestial

City soonest, but because he will escape many miseries that
the other will meet with in the rest of his journey." That is
all the comfort that Faithful has when he is shortly afterwards
scourged, lanced, pricked, stoned and burned to death.

We differ altogether from Bunyan as to what constitutes
sin.   He wants us to act like Christian, to sever domestic ties,
shun art, amusement, philosophic speculation, and to become
pious and ascetic.   He does not favor the intellectual or the
active life.   He thinks nothing of a view of life that has not
theology as its basis.   We find very little intellect in the
book.   The most intellectual passage is Mr. Money-Love's
answer to the problem as to whether a poor minister may not
alter some of his principles to get a greater benefice and
whether a merchant may not pretend to be more religious if
he might thus get more customers.   There is something Machiavellian in his reasoning and we almost approve it at heart.
The question under discussion is really whether it sometimes
is not proper to avoid fanaticism in one's views if such a
course will redound to the material benefit of a man.   And
those who know the instability of ideas may not be too hard
upon such folk who after all make up a large part of the
world.   People have become broad minded and do not inquire
to closely into every one's religious views in detail.

Some of the more liberal critics like Froude who admire
Bunyan try to show us that the allegory can be appreciated
by the free thinker as well as by the religious.   But the matter
and the form in the allegory are so closely blended that we can
scarcely disentangle them.   Bunyan tried to transmit certain
ideas and convictions and for this purpose uses his metaphors,
visions and character sketches.   We can select parts of the

book where there is little obtrusion of theology but on the whole there is little of secular and artistic value.

We do not find our experiences or lives related in the story. We are no longer like Christian. We find types of ourselves in portrayals of those who aim at a goal without being subject to religious ravings. We find ourselves in character studies of men who have a worthy ambition, who seek love, or crave for advancement, or reach out for justice or bear responsibilities. Occasionally a deluded revivalist comes along who creates anew people in the image of Christian.

There is a second part to the allegory published in 1684, six years after the first part. All are agreed that it is the inferior of the two parts of the book. It recounts the journey of Christiana, the wife of Christian, and their four children over the same territory that he traversed to reach the Celestial City. She blames herself, unjustly however, for not having gone with her husband, although he was the deserter. She takes the journey because she had a letter from her husband's King. In the second part we meet some new characters, like Great-Heart, who no doubt was drawn from one of Cromwell's soldiers. He is always fighting giants whom of course he vanquishes. There is a repetition of many incidents of the first part. There is much theology here and we have the children answering their catechism, although some pages later on we learn that they get married. The places visited by the new pilgrims are not as troublesome as they were to Christian. The interesting passages in the second part are few, and one of the best is the description of Madame Bubble who represents the world. She knows how to win friends, to get along comfortably, to turn aside misguided idealists from their quests. She makes people sell themselves and strive against one another. There are lacking in the second part the few merits we have in the first part. When we think of Bunyan's allegory we always think of Christian's progress and not of Christiana's.

In judging the book we must not be blinded by sympathy for the author. We know that the allegory was written in prison, in which the author languished for twelve years and from which he refused to be released on condition that he refrain from preaching. Nothing is more admirable than his courage and endurance; few men have gone through more poignant suffering. But he was deluded; hallucinations troubled him; his intelligence was very slight; he clung to the theological dogmas he imbibed; he never uttered an original idea; he invariably embraced a false view-point.

We are justified in saying then that the theme of Bunyan's work does not vitally touch us to-day. Although like him we are also pilgrims on a journey, we are bound for other goals and travel with different companions and traverse different places. We strive for freedom, for justice, for material help to ourselves and fellow men. We pursue culture, art, science, philosophy; we are engaged in a business, a profession or a trade. We do not wear on our sleeves a badge notifying everyone that we seek either a religious or a righteous life.

In Christian's world we find ourselves strangers. We must go back a few centuries and act and feel like the old Puritans, but we perceive that we become unnatural. In his world we are remote from our own times and from the times of the most cultured ages when the spirit of beauty and speculation was abroad. Here beauty is sin and we are forbidden to enjoy it. Alas! a pilgrimage is gone through with much suffering and

toil and for what? To live a life in which all that makes
it sweet is banned and all that is delusive is its goal. The
end striven for by Christian was death; he sought to know
how to die rather than how to live. When he reaches the
Celestial City he has become pure and sinless; the bitter lesson
is that death alone will free us from our sins. But we do not
deliberately seek death through wilful choice of suffering.
We accept pain and dissolution out of necessity, but do not
make a religion of them. We know moreover that his effort
after religious salvation is mere striving after a false ideal
that he had created for himself; no power within or outside
of nature demands that we make ourselves miserable to attain
unworthy goals.

Moreover allegory as a form of literature has passed away
and we do not care about bloodless types who are denominated
by the various vices and virtues. People in real life are
both good and evil, and literature to be true to life must
give us such types. In real life good does not always triumph,
whereas in allegory it must always do so. Then when alle-
gorizing extends to finding religious meanings in ordinary
natural events, the reader rebels. For instance when the
children of Christiana are being catechised, among the
answers are such as these: the springs come from the sea
to us through the earth to show us that the grace of God
comes to us through the body of Christ; some springs rise
out of the tops of high hills to show that the spirit of grace
will also spring up in the mighty as well as the lowly.

Bunyan's work does not for one instant deserve the fame it
has and Christian is not to be compared as a literary personage
with Gulliver or Robinson Crusoe and certainly not with Don
Quixote.

When one reflects that the allegory has been translated into about seventy-five languages and dialects, one is amazed that a work with so little of the eternal values should be so famous. The best argument against the intellectual poverty, the artistic barrenness and the moral and religious perniciousness of the book is that it has been successfully used by missionaries in converting cannibals, savages and heathens. It is distinctly a missionary's hand-book, and not a work of art. It reeks with error and falsehood, couched in alluring images, that there is little wonder it appeals to aborigines who are deficient in intelligence and morals. Nor should its wide appeal make one think that it has that touch of nature which makes the world akin. The story that children delight in the book and read it through is mythical; many children try to read it but usually drop it. If one believes that *Pilgrim's Progress* is an effective implement to be employed in spreading old-fashioned Christianity, let him use it for that purpose if he is bent that way. But let us abandon the notion that the vision written in Bedford Jail is one of the greatest of the world's literary master pieces.

A KEMPIS: THE IMITATION OF CHRIST

The *Imitation of Christ* is really an apology for the life of a monk and hence falls like an incomprehensible message upon our ears. It allows us to make no compromise even between the spiritual and temporal life; it impresses us as the work of a recluse who thought only of illusory things. One might take the words " Abandon all reality, ye who enter here " as the motto for this book. The author feels that we should exterminate our natural instinct; he enjoins upon us religious emotion to the exclusion of every other feeling; he seeks to base life upon a foundation of false ideas and useless morals and to convert the world into one large monastery.

Why should we imitate Jesus Christ? Why should millions of people pattern themselves after an ascetic and self-martyring idealist who lived in a different age and under different circumstances from our own. If the world were populated with Christ types we would have few great inventors, philosophers or scientists. Great industrial and diplomatic activities would be at a standstill. Why assume that there is no life without Jesus, when millions of pagans, Jews, Mohammedans, Buddhists, Confucians, and free-thinkers have led happy and rational existences without giving thought to him? The blind worship and grovelling humility of A Kempis before Christ alienates the reader. Take the following passage: " What can the world profit thee without Jesus? To be without Jesus is a grievous hell; and to be with Jesus, a sweet paradise. If Jesus be with thee no enemy shall be able to hurt thee.   He that findeth Jesus findeth a good treasure, yea, a good above all good.   And he that loseth Jesus loseth overmuch, yea more than the whole world.   Most poor is he who liveth without Jesus; and he most rich who is dear to Jesus." (Book II, Chap. VIII, Verse 2.)   A passage like this appeals to one whose credulity has been imposed upon.

Again take the last chapter of the second book entitled " Of the Royal Way of the Holy Cross."   The author obliges us to thrust ourselves into the pathway of pain.   But we feel convinced that life is not attained by courting agony.   The world should forget the cross, the symbol of martyrdom.   But when we hear a man shouting " In the cross is salvation, in the cross is life, in the cross is protection against our enemies, in the cross is infusion of heavenly sweetness, in the cross is strength of mind, in the cross joy of spirit, in the cross height of virtue, in the cross the perfection of sanctity," we marvel that the human spirit should apotheosize all that is antagonistic to it. We are told that all consists in the cross and that all lies in our dying on it and that there is no other way into life.   Yet thinkers have given us profound thoughts, poets have sung sublime songs, painters have given us soul stirring art-works, without the aid of the cross.   Scientists have wrested secrets from nature chiefly by deliberately throwing down the cross; men have led peaceful beautiful lives without being concerned about the cross.   A Kempis's extolling of suffering and death irritates us.   " Know for certain that thou oughtest to lead a dying life.   And the more any man dieth to himself, so much the more doth he begin to live unto God."   " Indeed if there had been any better thing, and more profitable to man's salvation than suffering, surely Christ would have showed it by word and example."   But we do not want to lead a dying life; we do not want salvation through pain; we do not wish to be coddled into welcoming suffering, into lauding all that is destructive of life.

The keynote to the book is in its detestation of nature. Not a word is said about a beautiful landscape, about feminine beauty; everything that is natural is condemned. It is absolutely an unnatural book. Grace is the be-all and end-all of existence. To pray to God, to abandon the world, to remove oneself from one's friends and acquaintances, to hate everything pleasurable, is what grace commands us. We are told man is created anew in the image of God when he completely subdues nature and is suffused with grace. A Kempis draws an interesting comparison between the different stirrings of nature and grace (Book III, Chap. IV). After reading it the reader feels that if A Kempis is right nature is a superfluity in the universe. It seems grace is not concerned with anything going on here; grace does not mind sorrow, contempt, ignorance; she is satisfied with things eternal and consolation in God alone. The reader wonders wherein are the crimes of nature because she is unwilling to die or to be kept down or subdued, because she strives for her own advantage, is willing to have some outward consolation, is disturbed about losses, likes leisure and prefers many other things which theology has censured but which are really laudable. Let grace have her treasure in heaven, let her lack curiosity for knowledge, let her delight in rough things; we will not quarrel with those whom she illuminates. But most men are so constructed as to shun her and to follow the promptings of nature. To act naturally and prudently is the heritage of all men; they will not heed admonitions to be otherwise than what they really are. A book like the *Imitation of Christ* encourages hypocrisy; we should not venerate a body of precepts that we know cannot be practised by a normal man. Life is to be enjoyed only by giving nature her due; and there are times we should reconcile our philosophy with our lives instead of conforming our conduct to the mandates of theology. The Christian of to-day does not lead an ascetic life nor does he advocate it; and the book does not represent modern Christianity.

A Kempis's zeal for praising God is so great that he deplores the necessity of spending some time eating, drinking and sleeping. "Would God there were not these necessities" he exclaims (Book. I, Chap. XXV, Verse 8). What is this contemplation of God, this being united to Him, this praying to Him? What is this word of God that man should always hearken to it? When A Kempis endeavors to attain the kingdom of heaven, he does nothing but seek to follow out some fallacious ethical precepts and to be obedient to some religious ceremonies all founded by man. This God-worship, this struggle towards God, is, as Feuerbach once pointed out, but self-worship and the attempt to realize human ideals. To be united with God really means to get into a state of ecstasy wherein you imagine that you have nothing human about you, wherein you think that you are almost the Lord yourself. But we can never get rid of the Adam within us, our bodies must cling to us even when we are in such ecstasy; the mark of the animal is always upon us. To obey the word of God means to do things that some people formerly said were holy; in other words the supposed word of God is nothing more than the word of man. The realization of the divine is but the achievement of something human. All the errors of antiquity are forced upon us by the statement that they emanate from

God. One finds every savage and every semi-civilized age attributes its unsupportable fabrications and crude conceptions to its deity. Mysticism resolves itself into something earthiest of the earthy. There is no word of God, no possibility of being suffused with God, no communion with or experience of God. Man worships his own ideals, and attributes them to a Creator. The kingdom of heaven is nothing more than a monk's paradise.

Yet there are instances where A Kempis moves us by the glowing warmth of his prayer, bespeaking the thousand agonies of his soul. It is apparent that he suffered from his seclusion, from his attempt to lead an unnatural life. As an instance let any one read the chapter called " Of the day of eternity and this life's straitness " (Book III, Chap. XLVIII). Its fervor is unsurpassed. It is a heart-breaking complaint of a frail mortal pleading for relief from sorrow. It shows a noble aspiration for an ideal, mistaken as that is; it pleads for security from wicked thoughts. It depicts the struggles he was constantly undergoing with himself and he here strikes a chord in our own hearts.

Nevertheless A Kempis makes little appeal to us. His contempt for knowledge, for the world, for humanity, render him an unsympathetic creature. We study him as a type of asceticism through his prayers and addresses. He is almost a different creature from ourselves; he is not possessed of our aspirations and ambitions; he does not seem to have our emotions, frailties, affections. He makes no mention of the love of the sexes; he rails against friendship; he is not interested in the domestic relations. Everything that makes life worth living is subject to his condemnation. Were we to follow his precepts we should experience no delights whatsoever. Were we to take his counsel we would stagnate intellectually and injure ourselves both materially and morally.

Yet liberal minded thinkers have bowed in reverence to this harmful author out of deference to authority. A free-thinker like George Eliot almost becomes fervid speaking about the *Imitation of Christ* in her *Mill on the Floss*. A positivist like Comte treasured the book highly and constantly had it by his side. How powerfully the opinions of ancient critics sway us! Here are two authors who separated themselves from belief in ascetic and dogmatic Christianity and they idolize a work that reeks with medievalism. They should have been among the first to emancipate themselves from worship of a book whose persistence gives superstition a strong weapon.

More controversies have arisen to solve the question of the authorship of the *Imitation of Christ* than of almost any other book. For three hundred years books and pamphlets have been written to establish the claims that have been made for Gersen, A Kempis and others. A whole library could be formed of publications which are concerned with this subject. What futile learning and patient research is often wasted on trite themes! It is profitless to expend scholarship on the question of the authorship of any book, even though a worthy one; how much more vanity is it to seek to determine who wrote a harmful and inartistic book!

The *Imitation of Christ* has been translated into over fifty languages and has gone through more than six thousand editions. It is almost incomprehensible. But hymn books and prayer books are being constantly reprinted. And as a matter of fact A Kempis's book is not literature at all but a religious handbook that has been palmed off upon us as a literary masterpiece. It is a book of devotion and not an æsthetic performance. Though the product of a Catholic, Protestants have also found much in it to satisfy them; in their editions they usually omit the fourth book on the Communion. This little volume written in Holland in the early part of the fifteenth century by the manuscript copyist A Kempis has probably done more to keep alive medieval dogma than any other book published since.

We listen to him and cannot help thinking of our Darwin. We read and yet cannot rid ourselves of remembrances of our studies in comparative religion. We feel the promptings of our physical faculties and wonder why the author wants us to resist them. He appears to us like a visitor from some other planet.

To-day we ask men to lead good and useful lives; we do not think it wrong to better one's condition; we only ask that people should not wilfully and needlessly pain their neighbor. We admit that A Kempis also struggles for a high moral ideal, but it is a useless and often pernicious one. He lays more stress on religious ecstasy and prayer and church rites than on a purely moral life. When he does laud humility he never dreams that it is of earthly growth just as pride is and that there is nothing divine about it. He is obsessed by the notion that he is closer to God when on his knees in his chamber than when out in the open field observing the beauty of nature. We say to ourselves, "This man is mad for he is living constantly in delusions. He mistakes the figments of his brain for realities. The book is a madman's Bible."

No doubt the *Imitation of Christ* still brings consolation to many, it still takes off a weary load from the minds of many of its readers. But it can help only those who subscribe to effete dogma; the reader must be intellectually fettered to reap the full benefits of perusing this work. The scholar may find something in the book that appeals to him. For he, like the monk, also lives a secluded life, devoted to his ideal and scorning the world. But he does not necessarily pursue phantoms nor does he give up the world because it is a sinful one. He studies in solitude because he is really an epicurean; he gives up minor pleasures for a great one.

The book insists upon our renouncing our will, upon our suppressing our individuality, upon our stifling our abilities. We suffer many of our misfortunes because we cannot will, because we cannot bravely assert our personalities. We should, therefore, not lavish praises upon a book that encourages us in our weakness in developing our will power. It may no doubt be prudent to crush our will for that which is beyond our power, but to ask us to root out our desires for things that we can attain by a slight exertion, is unfair. We are creatures of flesh and blood and in us have been planted certain instincts, like that of love for knowledge, art, honor, riches and beauty, and it is useless to tell us that we should have contempt for all the things of this world in order to tend towards the kingdom of heaven.

The book preaches everything that is opposed to the best in Greek and modern authors. It tells us that the more we can get out of ourselves, the more divine will we be; they tell us that the more we can be ourselves the more will we approach the divine. The *Imitation* maintains that the less we rely on ourselves and the more we adopt the ideas of others, the nobler will we be. Greek and modern literature recognize that we can only cultivate the best that is in us by trusting solely in ourselves. A Kempis repeatedly asserts human nature to be vile, man to be full of sin, not worth comfort or consolation.

Greater authors and deeper thinkers and higher moralists teach us that human nature is not vile, that man is to be treated as dignified.

"The scheme of the book," said Thackeray, "if carried out would make the world a wretched dreary place of sojourn. There would be no manhood, no love, no tender ties of mother and child, no use of intellect, no trade or science, a set of selfish beings crawling about avoiding one another, and howling a perpetual misérére."

The author goes so far as to say that even after we have given everything of ourselves, completely renounced all the pleasures of this world and entirely suppressed our own individualities, even then we have done nothing. It is at a point like this one loses patience with the philosophy of life laid down and critical examination must stop.

ST. AUGUSTINE: CONFESSIONS

The *Confessions* of St. Augustine has been his most permanent literary performance. It appeals to many not because of the abundant theology coursing through it but as a psychological document showing the workings of the mind and spirit of a man who is undergoing the process of conversion. It has come down to us as a monument to a sinner who, trying all creeds, embraced Christianity and became the most able and influential of the Fathers of the Church. It finds among its admirers critics who accept nothing of Augustinism, but are attracted by the story of its author's misdeeds, by the account of his intellectual wanderings and final conversion, by his tale of motherly devotion and by some of his reflections on secular subjects.

Yet the reader who is aware of what baneful influence St. Augustine has been in spreading many false and pernicious views, would prefer that he had never been converted. He did much to ruin the intellectual standpoint of humanity and to plunge Europe into the dark ages. He indulged in more fruitless controversies and speculated on more useless problems and gave more absurd solutions to questions than most of his contemporaries. He added so much dogma to the simple moral precepts of Christianity and he was the predecessor of the scholastic philosophers.

His *Confessions* is distinctly old-fashioned Christian literature and must necessarily appeal most to faithful medieval Christians. To the adherent of any other religion or the

person emancipated from all revealed religion it presents few
attractions.   A certain measure of sympathy with its views
is necessary to awaken appreciation for the book.   It has had
an unhealthy influence in driving men into religious mania,
and it has founded a whole school of literature, namely the
books containing accounts of sinners and criminals who were
reformed by accepting dogmas.   One hears the voice of St.
Augustine in the speeches of Salvation Army speakers.   One
hears it in frenzied and fanatical revivalists who go about
driving whole communities mad.   One finds an analogy
between him and a man like Tolstoi, who ruined his art
because he turned his mind to religion for solace for his early
sins.

One thing that makes the *Confessions* tedious is that the
book is addressed directly to God, and not to the reader.   The
author talks with the Creator as if He were a priest to whom
he is is confessing his sins.   He cringes before Him and coaxes
Him.   He assumes that God is interested in every step that
he takes; so he flatters Him and lavishes compliments upon
Him.   He feels that God is a pious Christian who is greatly
concerned because men want to follow out their natural instincts and enjoy life.   He loves the Creator as though He were
flesh and blood and expects Him to cease from His work in
speeding on the universe to absorb Himself in St. Augustine.
His Deity is always disapproving of something or other.   We
become offended with the fawning apologies of the author.
We want God removed from the book and not to interfere
with the story that the sinner has to tell.   And those who do
not accept the theory of a personal God who is sitting up in the
heavens and growing angry because religious and moral sinners
exist, feel that St. Augustine is talking in vain, that no one

hears him, that no power cares the least whether he had been converted or not, that no supernatural agency is weighing every deed of his. The bringing in of God has spoiled the *Confessions* as a piece of literature.

God takes no more concern about us than he does about the lower creatures from whom we are descended. Everything demonstrates that there is no special power outside of nature herself, taking a particular interest in mankind. We believe that men are not being specially watched by such a power, that we live out our lives in accordance with eternal and immutable laws which have made us what we are, that we have evolved through pre-existing conditions by necessity and that no mind has purposely designed our physical or moral nature. The God who has the human qualities most lauded by man like love, intelligence, power, righteousness, does not exist. He was invented by man as an embodiment of ideals which man would like to see prevail. The God who created this universe out of nothing, who may be induced by prayer to violate the laws of nature, to interfere in our affairs and forward our happiness, who is angry when men sin and wants virtue to triumph and who asks us to accept Christ as His son is a chimera.

There is no doubt that the two most admired books of the *Confessions* are the eighth and the ninth, the former containing the account of St. Augustine's conversion and the latter the story of his mother Monica and of her death.

He was converted by hearing of how others less learned than himself embraced Christianity through their reading of St. Anthony, the Egyptian monk. He began to see how crooked, defiled, spotted and ulcerous he was and he marvelled that the unlearned thus took heaven by force while he with his learning wallowed in flesh and blood. Then he did much weeping;

he imagined that God was angry at him for his sins; remorse
stirred him; he heard a voice telling him to take up and read
and then he read the passage telling him to put on the Lord
Jesus Christ and not to make provision for the flesh.   But the
seeds of his conversion had been sown in him as a child when
his mother instilled the lessons of Christ in him.   His nature
was essentially a religious nature; he found difficulty recon-
ciling this with his wanton life.   He had mistresses, one of
whom bore him a child.   It was partly a guilty conscience
that influenced him in his conversion.   He needed theology
to purify him morally; otherwise he would have remained
riotous.

We sympathise with his sincerity and his desire to find
truth and to reform, but we know that he is deluded.   He
would not live a temperate life unless he felt that God was
pleased with him and would reward him in the future.   He
did not love goodness for itself, but because it was pleasing
to Christ.   He needed as an example the story of a monk
like St. Anthony to persuade him that life should not consist
only of physical pleasure.   He had to know that God sent His
son down to die for him, before he would lead a moral life.
St. Augustine is the type of the well meaning but misguided
sinner who regrets his misdeeds and needs religion alone to
reform him.

The world has had too many of these stories of conversions
to dogmatic religion.   It needs more accounts of people who
have been emancipated from it, of men who have thrown over
the shackles of superstition which bound them.   Let us have
the tales of those who braved their times and defied their
friends and stood out clear of all the theological trappings
that bound them.   Let us listen to the cries of relief of

people who, having lived in religious error, became " heretical "
and refused to continue walking in darkness. We would
rather peruse the story of the sinner, if sinner we must have,
who tells us that he was reformed by the desire no longer to
afflict others with pain, by a growing love of righteousness for
its own sake. We are not aware that morality must be taught
by means of theology to everybody.

As a result of his conversion St. Augustine gave up teaching oratory and devoted himself to God. We see his intellectual dissolution immediately. He becomes a believer in
two very common errors in the Middle Ages, one in the power
of prayer to cure disease and the other in the efficacy of a touch
of the corpse of a saint to cure blindness. He tells us in all
seriousness how when stricken with the toothache he asked his
friends to pray for him and how as soon as they bowed their
knees, the pain disappeared. He also relates that, when a
blind man touched with his handkerchief the bier of two
recently exhumed martyrs, his eyes were opened immediately.
If St. Augustine previously believed these events could not
have occurred, is it not to be regretted that his mental powers
should have been so weakened by his conversion as to make
him place credence in these miracles?

St. Augustine shows more of the human touch in his great
love for his mother. His grief moves us, but the type of
woman for which Monica stands is not admirable. She is a
patient Griselda type and represents the woman who admitted
that she was her husband's slave and did not complain about
his wrongs to her. She allowed her husband to wrong her
bed, and she never resisted him when angry, even by word.
She told other women that they were really servants after they
were married and that they should not set themselves up

against their lords. She was fanatical on the subject of religion. She was willing to die now that her supreme desire, the conversion of her son to Christianity, had been accomplished. As an instance of her wisdom her son tells of a reply she gave to some who wanted to know if she were not afraid when away from her own city. " Nothing is far to God," she said, " nor was it to fear lest at the end of the world He should not recognize whence He were to raise me up."

Before dying she used to discuss the eternal life with her son. Nothing of this earth that was most delightful to the earthly senses could be compared to the sweetness of that life. One ponders on this spectacle of mother and son mutually encouraging one another in illusions and yet one cannot help but loving them. When Monica finally dies, her son for a while forgets his religion; the natural man breaks out and we have a masterly recital of a son's grief for the death of his mother. There is no one who will not sympathise with him here. There is something naïve about his trust in God when he prayed to Him to heal his sorrows; and as God did not do so, the bereaved man concluded that even though he now fed upon no deceiving word, still the Lord wanted to impress upon him how strong is the bond of all habit.

The asceticism of St. Augustine is the natural reaction which theology has brought upon a man who once loved life and study. He now looks upon all learning that has not God as its subject as fruitless. He asks what profit did the reading of so-called liberal books procure him. He knew rhetoric, music and mathematics, but he did not thence sacrifice to God. In fact they helped him on the road to perdition since he did not keep his strength for God. He mentions his studies in Cicero and Aristotle, but they were defective to him because they did not mention Christ nor help him to define God. He regrets having striven after theatrical applause and poetical prizes; he is even sorry that he witnessed shows. He now formed theories of life entirely in conflict with his pleasure-loving nature. He who formerly loved fame concluded that to want to be loved by one's fellow creatures for the joy therein was evidence of a miserable life and foul boastfulness.

He decides that he must not allow his senses to make him happy as enjoyment was sinful. He does not want his eyes to love fair and varied forms and bright and soft colors; he wants God to occupy his soul instead, for He made these things. He seeks not to have any pleasures from eating, smelling, hearing. He regrets that men make certain adornments in their clothes, that they make pictures to tempt their eyes. People follow these artistic products which they themselves make and neglect God who made them. He objects to the trait of curiosity which leads men to search out the hidden power of nature. A large portion of the tenth book is taken up with a statement of his ascetic ideals and one is saddened to know that the effect of conversion has been to make a student of philosophy, an author of an æsthetic treatise, hate both knowledge and beauty. He attacks pleasures which no one thinks reprehensible. We do not have to defend the right of the eye, ear and nostrils to enjoy their natural functions. Yet the man who admits that he once practised some unnatural vices sets himself up as a censor of all natural forms of enjoyment.

He is too stern and when he blames himself for simple boyish faults we are amused. Of course he cried when his elders did not accede to his wishes; he neglected his studies and played games; he liked to hear stories and see shows; he committed

petty thefts at home and told lies. Though he complains of
being beaten and blames elder people for similar vices on a
larger scale he makes too much of his wickedness. He even
deplores the fact that he wept at the story of Dido's love for
Æneas and did not think of weeping at his own want of love
for God.

However the *Confessions* is not altogether the tale of a
sinner. St. Augustine draws a curtain over much that would
interest us; he may be sincere but he is neither frank nor
honest. One looks in vain for a really true picture of an un-
blushing sinner. He tells us that he stole pears as a boy and
moralizes beautifully over the deed. He did not want the pears
and even threw them away; he loved the company and the sport.
But the theft took place in his sixteenth year. He had a
concubine by whom he had a son and then when she was torn
away he took another, but a few short paragraphs tell of his
illicit relations. He does not say anything about these women
nor of his relations with them. Women meant so much to
him as a young man and yet he passes them by. He never
entertains us with vivid realistic accounts of his sins. He
has not the courage or openness of a Rousseau. He does not
dwell for any length on any event that tends to incriminate
him. He just mentions his sin, but what the reader misses is
the graphic account of his wrong-doings.

The *Confessions* is really a history of his intellectual development. He was in turn a Manichean, a sceptic, a Neo-Platonist
and a Christian. We pity him as he shows himself in the
throes of doubt, always taking up something new and then
finding a reason for discarding it. That he ended by accepting
dogma is only proof that he needed authority to compel him
to hold steadfast by his doctrines. The man of ever fluctuat-

ing opinions either becomes a Nihilist, believing nothing, or
he attaches himself to a creed and accepts everything that it
sanctions.   We are not interested in the trite reasons he gives
for dropping and accepting various beliefs; but we love to
observe his ever wavering mind.

He read some Neo-Platonists and found that they identified
the Word or Logos with God.   But Neo-Platonism was for
St. Augustine really a step towards Christianity because of its
emphasis on idealism.   Neo-Platonism taught the existence
of the spiritual without the accompaniment of the material.
However this system of philosophy to-day is rejected by many
thinkers and moreover is not used as a means of defending
Christianity.   There is no doubt that St. Augustine would
have become converted had he never heard of Neo-Platonism.
What attracted him about Christianity was the idea of the
atonement; the clause " the Word was made flesh " meant for
him that God descended upon the earth in the body of Christ.

The doctrines that had the strongest hold on St. Augustine
were those of Manicheism.   He attacks these continually
just because they had held him in thrall.   The reasons he
advances for abandoning the views of the Manicheans may not
be convincing; he found some astronomical errors in their
books and was disillusioned with one of their teachers, Faustus.
Manicheism with its theories of light and darkness and good
and evil fighting each other is a dead issue.   There are many
pages in his book on the subject of Manicheism and they do
not form entertaining reading.

As a story of intellectual development the *Confessions* is
trivial; we find retrogression rather than progress.   We like
the St. Augustine who read his Cicero and Aristotle, who
enjoyed shows and loved life.   We regret that he never carried

out his plan of becoming a disciple of Epicurus instead of drifting off into theology. He might have embraced a philosophy which taught that the gods do not interfere in the doings of man and lay up no tormenting Hades for him; instead St. Augustine adopted a belief which taught that God sets the laws of nature at rest for his favorite, man, and yet prepares a monstrous hell where people suffer for eternity. He held wisdom in the hollow of his hand and lo, it evaporated! He records the sad tale of his intellectual decline and believes he has received an acquisition of divine wisdom. He plunges into darkness and superstition and imagines he has found the way to eternal bliss. He never realizes that he has become a fallen creature, that he is now inferior to those thinkers whom he once venerated and whom he now holds in contempt.

There is something cowardly about the man that is apparent throughout the *Confessions*. We see this cowardice in the account he gives us of his desertion of his mother after he had persuaded her to wait for him all night. We see it in his refusal to state the nature of the crime he committed in church and for which he deserved death, according to his own judgment. He refrained from carnal pleasure only because he feared the Lord's punishment. He abandoned the sinful life because he felt assured that he would thus get into the grace of God and attain the blessed abodes of heaven.

The *Confessions* is of interest chiefly to the student of religious phenomena. Those who like to study the repentant temperament from the psychological point of view will be interested in this work. Those who, instead of trying to root out error, prefer to study it and apologise for it will find ample opportunity for doing so in this autobiography. But the critic who does not wish to encourage countless repetitions of

a similar evolution to puerile doctrines will not look sympathetically upon the story of St. Augustine's conversion. We
should condemn the triumph of undoubted falsehood and not
be forever trying to explain it away. We may exclaim that
all such phenomena as religious conversion are to be accounted
for by enviroment, disposition and other causes, but we must
also consider the question whether such conversion is worthy
of our approval; whether it does not make a man deteriorate.

The *Confessions,* while it relates events unconnnected with
dogma such as the author's friendship with Alypius, is on the
whole ruined by theology. The last four of the thirteen books
particularly are unreadable and are omitted in some editions.
We are called upon to applaud the spectacle of a noble mind
overthrown by dogma; we are asked by the author to place
full faith in his theological tenets; he recounts his adventures
only for the purpose of converting us also. But we are unable
to feel with him. We know that his conversion was one of the
greatest calamities in the history of the world. He kept civilization back for many centuries; his evil influence still goes
on. Besides the autobiographies of Goethe or Rousseau or
Cellini his story is insignificant.

PASCAL: THOUGHTS

Pascal's book *Thoughts* was posthumously published in 1670 about eight years after its author's death. These reflections were jotted down irregularly and we have them chiefly in fragmentary form. They were intended to be an apology for the Christian religion. There are sceptical ideas here and there which show the influence of Montaigne. But it is no longer customary to regard Pascal as a freethinker. He is now regarded by many critics as one of the great bulwarks of Christianity. We know that he believed in the dogmas that are part of the Christian religion. He was ascetic in his outlook upon life and disapproved of pleasure and diversion.

It is true Pascal admits at times that we cannot actually prove the truth of the Christian religion or the existence of a God. His chief proof, which is really a negation of proof, is that in matters like these the heart is a better guide than the head. He is willing to trust to his instincts; he is confident that he cannot err here. He assumes that he would not have been made to feel instinctively that the Christian religion was true had it not been so. He claims that the heart gives us knowledge of first principles, that we know for instance there are three dimensions in space and that numbers are infinite, not through our reason, but by instinctive knowledge. This of course is not so. We may feel something instinctively to-day but back in the distant ages it was a process of reasoning which made our ancestors accept particular conclusions. There was a reason once assigned for every belief; we continue clinging to the theory long after we have discovered the fallacy of

the arguments that originally supported it.   A former method
of thinking influences us in our " instinctive " feeling to-day.

To call upon the heart as justification for a belief is the last
resort of one who admits that his faith appears hopeless from
the point of view of reason.   The savage who believes in idols
may argue in the same manner as Pascal does.   Belief in
witchcraft, ghosts, devils was originally supported by proof
and finally became part of the instinctive knowledge of some
people.   We feel assured of the " truth " of certain matters
that are really false, only because our emotions have been
trained and prejudiced to feel that way for ages.   A Moham-
medan or Jew does not feel in his heart that God had a son
who had to die to save mankind.   Just as one's conscience
may annoy him if he has transgressed some trivial religious
rites because it had been formed that way by many ages of
religious education, so one may feel that the false religion
he was born in is veracity itself.

It is true, the emotions are often the only guide for us.   A
man who is hungry does not reason that he ought to eat any
more than does one who comes in contact with something that
causes him pain, argue that he ought to withdraw his body
from the obnoxious object.   Here instinct is a true guide.
But how different from that of which Pascal speaks, which is
to reveal to us truth in intellectual matters !   It does not follow
that everything my heart would like to believe is true.   I
naturally want to converse with the dead ones I love, but I
cannot be sure that I will do so because I am so inclined.   I
may be disappointed with the injustice in this world, but that
does not prove that there must be another perfect world, because
I feel there should be one.   Let us face the truth that nature

does not concern herself with our desires nor take any suggestions from us as to how this universe should be conducted.

So it is untrue to say that the heart and not the reason proves to us the truth of Christianity and the existence of a personal God; that the heart should be trusted in its adoption of faith; that we should try to know things not by the effort of the understanding but by the simple submission of the reason. No doubt the mind is limited, but that is no excuse for believing what is utterly repugnant to it. It is our guide in dismissing absurdities even though it does not disclose to us all knowledge.

One of the most famous passages in Pascal shows us that we ought to accept God, by means of the analogy of a wager. He says that by believing in a God one has everything to gain and nothing to lose, that we should prefer risking our single brief life for the possibility of gaining eternity. Pascal holds that it is better to be on the safe side and to adopt a belief in which there is no harm and possibly rewards for accepting it. You may suffer an eternity of pains by being a non-believer, so do not undertake the risk. But other religious sects tell us we are lost if we do not accept their dogmas and the gods and the leaders whom they worship. They also may apply the analogy of the wager in making us adopt their faiths. But why should I be placed in the position of forcing a belief upon myself because its upholders start with premises which I reject from the start. One may as well make me believe in demons and mythical creatures by telling me that it is most advisable not to doubt their existence, since if they do exist they may torture me after I am dead. To frighten one into a religion is the most primitive way of spreading it, but fear does not have any effect upon those who immediately sweep away certain conclusions. If the wager theory governed us in making us receive articles of faith it could be utilized for any creed and indeed for all absurdities that have sprung up in the breasts of mankind. Many critics have dismissed the wager-idea of Pascal with a shake of the head.

The keynote of Pascal's religion is the corruption of human nature; he dwells on it constantly; he has not the slightest doubt that man is fallen from a higher state and is vile. He admits that we cannot conceive the transmission of Adam's sin to us but he is satisfied that we are miserable and corrupt and that we can be saved by Jesus. He admits it is unjust that we should suffer for Adam's sin and yet asserts that without this mystery we are incomprehensible to ourselves, and that God has concealed the knot which would untie this mystery, to render the difficulty of our existence more unintelligible to us. Thus Pascal simply makes statements which have nothing to support them and adopts as the corner-stone of his religion an exploded dogma. He tries to balance our corruption with a certain divinity that he says exists in us. Now man is neither divine nor corrupt. He is not a fallen creature nor can he ever rise to be a god. He has evolved from lower creatures, is a natural product of nature just as all other living creatures are, and he calls that sin which either causes pain to some one or violates a custom.

Pascal is fascinated by the two extremes in man's nature, his corruption and his capability of being saved. He comments on both the brutishness and greatness of man. He maintains that only through the Christian religion does man learn his true state. But the reader wonders whither all this dogmatizing leads, what it solves. Man will continue as before to satisfy his natural desires, seek diversion and think on subjects that are of material interest to him. The greatness of a religion is not proved by its assumption that man is vilest of the vile and yet may become divine.

If Pascal had only known that we have the marks of the brute upon us even more than he imagined and that we possess still in our bodies rudimentary organs which we once used in a wild stage! If he could but have known that in spite of our animal nature most of us do not consider ourselves corrupt and born in sin but decent though imperfect! We try to avoid paining a neighbor purposelessly and transgressing against our sense of justice. In the future no system of thought will interest us that is based on the fundamental corruption presumed to be in man. People are probably more the victims of stupidity, convention and necessity than actually wicked for the mere sake of being wicked.

Pascal tried to defend miracles that we cannot accept. We know he believed that his niece's disease of the eye was cured by a touch from the thorn of the crown which it was supposed that the savior had worn. He held that the best proof of the Biblical miracles was in the very fact that there had been made false claims for other miracles which were not true. He is wroth at those who deny the virgin birth and resurrection as if they were impudent. He thinks when he tells us that a hen lays eggs without a cock, he has answered the objection of the virgin birth, but he omits to state that the hen's eggs will not hatch. He thinks he demolishes the disbelief in resurrection by asking whether birth is not more miraculous than a return to one's being. Theologians to-day do not use Pascal's arguments in support of miracles.

His views on Jesus Christ are medieval. To him Christ is the center to which all tends; he who knows Christ knows

the reason of all things.   Pascal abhors any one who seeks
God apart from Jesus.   We know God only by Jesus and by
Him we prove God.   We know ourselves by Jesus Christ and
apart from Christ we know neither life nor death nor God
nor ourselves.   In short Christ is God Himself.   Our prayers
and virtues are abominations before God if they are not of
Jesus Christ.   Pascal dislikes the deist as well as the atheist.
Thus Pascal descends into theology and much of his *Thoughts*
is not within the sphere of literature.

How weak are his arguments against the sceptics!   Indeed
he occasionally and unintentionally gives arguments in favor
of their views, hence it was concluded by some that he was a
freethinker.   He tries to use arguments that are against his
faith in support of it.   The fact that there are more religions
than one, is used by him to show that only one religion, the
Christian, can be true; for if there were only one religion it
would have been too easily recognized! The truth of religion
can be seen, according to Pascal, in its very obscurity, in the
little light we have of it and in our indifference to accepting
it.   God has willed to hide Himself from some because they
are unworthy, and He has revealed Himself to others.   There
is no reason for all this except that so He willed.   But most
people are justified in believing that when a religion is given
to save mankind and a redeemer is sent down, the eyes of men
should have been opened by that very God who wished to save
them.   Nor should that God conceal His true creed among
other false ones so that it should be difficult for men to know
which is the true one.   Why should God endeavor to save men
and yet set up obstacles that might have been easily removed?
Alas, Pascal does not understand that all religions have grown
up in the same way, that they represent the ideals of their

creators, that they are all fitted in part for those who believe in them and that they all abound in some falsehoods. He does not see that it matters little to Nature what men believe and that some religions are ruining men whom they are supposed to be saving, and he does not understand it is man who has made God in his own image. Yet he occasionally bestirs himself and exclaims that his proofs are not conclusive. He admits that he does not see everywhere the marks of a Creator although he is sure of the divinity of Christ. He confesses that even the proofs of Christianity are not convincing, but not unreasonable; still he undertakes to defend belief in the supernatural. He is inferior intellectually to Montaigne and Spinoza because they cast dogma and revelation aside.

His mind delighted in paradoxes and contradictions and we see that he has accepted his beliefs beforehand and then sought proof for them instead of being led to them by evidence. Not many came so near grasping the truth and then let it elude them. The very reflections that drove others to discard dogma persuaded him to cling to it all the closer. Even the existence of evil was used by him to defend religion. He saw man's position in the universe and perceived man's failings as a thinking being and he therefore concluded that Christ was divine and had to save man. No one was keener and yet more illogical than Pascal.

When he compared man's rank in nature to a nonentity as contrasted with infinity, to a universe contrasted with a nonentity, we wonder how Pascal could entertain the idea that man is the be-all and end-all of this universe, that God Himself died for him. Pascal looked out mentally into remotest corners of the universe; he contemplated the most invisible atom. Yet he could not perceive man was but a link in the chain of nature and that vanity makes him believe that he is an exception to all the natural laws. Pascal held some liberal philosophic views but nevertheless adopted reactionary theological conceptions.

He intended to be an apologist for Christianity but he really did not advance any plausible and convincing argument in its favor. He simply concluded that he felt this belief must be true. He even refused to accept proofs of religion from the works of nature herself. He did a service to mankind in rejecting such testimony but he did not realize what a weapon he put in the hands of sceptics when he stated that to try to prove the existence of a God from the works of nature herself shows religion has but weak proofs. He also maintains that in the attempt to prove God's existence metaphysically we see the evil results of trying to learn of God without Christ, to communicate with God without a mediator. Every argument men have used to prove God's existence he finds faulty and he does not present any stronger one himself. How illogical it is to say we cannot prove God's existence and then to assert we need Christ to know Him without showing conclusively first that we can know Him through Christ; nature should at least testify to the existence of God in Christ, if she does not to that of God.

What inane conclusions he arrived at when he wondered about the riddle of man's existence! He feels that there is an eternity and that man should not be indifferent to it. He argues thus: Perhaps torments face you; this life is very likely a preparation for a future life; it may be a dream from which we will awake in death. The immortality of the soul is an established fact and people should be thinking about it all the time. It is not proper that we should act as we often do if the soul is immortal. How stupid must be the man who does not reflect what will become of him! In short when Pascal troubles himself with these questions he does it with his mind perverted by works on theology. He does it with a certain morbidity, he becomes pathological and we cannot enter into his way of feeling.

Men to-day are willing to place confidence in the scheme of things and to take for granted that they will not be damned. We wish to have our lives here free from pain and believe that we should not ascribe a deliberately evil purpose to nature when she really has none at all. We feel that in love and nature and art we have our delights and we do not want to be groaning needlessly about futile fears. Why let Pascal persuade us to inflict misery upon ourselves? Why let him give to us, under the pretext of trying to stir us up into philosophic speculation as to our destiny, the cruelest and falsest inventions of religious maniacs, a belief in a hell? We are not, like Pascal, miserable because we don't know what may become of us after death. He is aware that in trying to arouse us to think about our future after death he employs the strongest weapon that was instrumental in winning men to religion in the past. But we do not believe that nature thinks mankind or the church important enough for her to lay up a special hell for men who have not led a life sanctioned by the church. Pascal does not for a moment suspect that what won't happen to animals may not happen to man. Nay, he finds that when men reason out that they should be indifferent to the question of their future life, this in itself redounds to the glory of religion and strengthens it.

Pascal does not appeal to us when he criticises us for seeking diversions, when he would hinder us from finding joy in

life. He claims that pleasure and sport are deceptive for we
indulge in them to forget ourselves and to avoid thinking of
our destiny. But the only realities in life are the joys that
we experience, the love we feel, the good we accomplish, the
work we perform. Let the unseen world take care of itself. It
may have suited the unfortunate Pascal to complain that his
sister derived too much pleasure in loving her child; it may
have pleased him to torture himself by wearing an iron girdle
with spikes which he occasionally pressed to hurt him. But
we know that he made a philosophy out of his love of pain.
He worshipped sickness thinking it the natural state of a
Christian. Sickness was to him a blessing for it naturally
made him shun all worldly passions. We can then understand
why he hates the theater and all other amusements. Nor
does he believe in love at all. He wants you to love only God,
and not your fellow creatures; he thinks whatever is pleasing
to man is obnoxious to God. He did not want to enjoy eating;
he made a blessing out of poverty; he felt an aversion to his
former studies in science and mathematics because they did
not refer to nor were concerned with God.

One learns how faithful a believer, how literal a Christian
Pascal was on reading his prayer for the right use of sickness,
and his·views on death, when his father died. These essays
appear in some editions of the *Thoughts*. He does not look
upon death as natural but as something imposed upon men to
expiate their sins. Death is no evil but is really the beginning of life. Death with Jesus Christ is a joy, lovely and
holy. Death is not natural nor the result of necessity but of
a decree of Divine Providence, pre-ordained by God, etc.
What a perversion of the human mind! There is hardly anything like it in literature. Pascal deliberately allowed others

inferior to him intellectually to do his thinking for him and to foist upon him such mad views.

Also note the passionate prayer where he is imagining that some deity is angry with him for leading a perfectly natural life. He looks to God as to an unreasonable tyrant and he prostrates and humiliates himself before Him and attributes to deity a character that is outrageous and brutal. God is to Pascal a punisher of sinners and nothing else. He may be appeased by prayer and then send down His grace. Pascal prays neither for health nor life nor sickness nor death but for anything that might be advantageous to God's glory and his own salvation. Why should sickness be necessary to increase God's glory or Pascal's salvation? Why shout to this deity as if one were a contemptible worm and ask to be forgiven for things about which the deity is not concerned? Poor Pascal! how tragically sincere he was in this prayer! How it distils pain, yet how it seethes with loathsome doctrines! He does not ask for exemption from pain but for religious consolation along with his pain.

Many of Pascal's proofs rest on the Scriptures themselves. He does not regard them as a series of books written by men at different times and liable to error. Of course he considers the world a few thousand years old and finds proof of the creation in this way. "Shem, who saw Lamech, who saw Adam, saw also Jacob, who saw those who saw Moses." He believes that Adam was the witness and guardian of the promise concerning the savior and that many other characters in the Old Testament had a supernatural power in being able to describe him and foretell his existence. Pascal should not have tried to prove his case by falling back on the Bible, for those who accept it as the word of God need nothing else to convince them; and those who look upon it as a collection of ancient literature and not a book of Divine Revelation repudiate Pascal's examples from it.

He thinks because some philosophers are mistaken in their views and others admit their inability to solve all problems, that therefore philosophy is a failure and will not console man. He forgets that what he himself does is to accept theology instead of philosophy and probably because it impudently claims to know the answers to the most mysterious questions, whereas it is really far more mistaken than most systems of philosophy. But to some people the rational ideas of great thinkers are more consoling and give them more of an insight into truth than theology.

Many cultured people have no faith in revealed religion, although they have many emotions in common with religious people. They may be impressed with the helplessness of man in the face of calamities; with his blind despair when confronted with the death of those he loves. Almost every intelligent person at times wonders about the riddle of existence and tries some solution. Many must pray to a personal God who, they think, will ward off their calamities and then probably give them eternal life. Others find their ideas and feelings expressed in books by great thinkers, in art, in music.

The leading objections that Pascal brings against philosophers is probably better shown in the " Conversation of Pascal with M. De Saci on Epictetus and Montaigne," which is printed in some editions of the *Thoughts*. The Stoics attributed greatness to human nature while the Epicureans and sceptics attributed weakness to it; contrarieties were placed in the same subject. Now faith places them in different subjects, infirmity is placed in man and power in God. There-

fore both sects should accept the gospel because it will satisfy
the love of greatness in the Stoic sect by showing them that a
God has died for them and it will satisfy the other two sects
by showing them the corruption of man through sin.   Therefore both will find the truth in the gospel.   Pascal shows us
here his strongest argument against philosophy and for Christianity.   It appears again and again in different forms throughout the *Thoughts*.

How impotent it is we can readily see.   The existence of
religion does not depend on the greatness or littleness of human
nature.   A religion is not true just because it teaches that man
is corrupt and can be made great.   A religion is not true because
it contains on an exaggerated scale the germs of the leading
idea in two different and opposite schools of philosophy.   People
may believe that man has faults or that he is often grand,
without therefore accepting a faith that teaches man was
once perfect and fell and that he may again become great by
accepting a God who died for him.   And then it matters not
whether man is little or great.   Men have their limitations
and powers, and religion cannot increase the one nor diminish
the other.   The greatness and littleness of man have nothing
at all to do with the question as to whether there is a God or
not and what His nature is.

Pascal's system does not take into consideration merit but
grace.   A man cannot be saved by his own deeds and virtues
but by Divine Grace.   Nor can man help being corrupt no
matter how good and great he is.   Pascal even sought to make
us believe, by asking us to start with some religious rites like
taking holy water and having masses said, even though we did
not believe in them.

Still he is rich in general ideas and these are among his more valuable and permanent thoughts. When he thinks for himself and does not refer to theology, we get profound views that still sway us. No one worshipped thought more than Pascal, no one felt its dignity more. He has given us some ideas that have become part of the world's way of thinking and yet they do not savor of his religion. We are all familiar with his comparison of man to a thinking reed, who is more noble than a universe which would destroy him because he would know that he is dying while the universe would not know what it is achieving. It is Pascal who said that if the nose of Cleopatra had been shorter, the face of the world had been changed, and if there hadn't been a grain of sand in Cromwell's bladder a new dynasty and religion would have prevailed. In short when Pascal does not write as an apologist for religion he is still vital. Critics have congratulated themselves that he never finished his main theme and gave us his philosophic views first.

But nevertheless his real intention as an apologist overshadowed his secular thoughts. We admire and love him, but we feel that he is already largely obsolete. " We cannot follow him without treason to our highest interests," said Leslie Stephen of him. We are interested in his pains and in the fact that he set up an ideal for himself even though it is not our own. We watch a fellow creature troubled about some things that do not disturb many of us. We know of his great physical sufferings and our heart bleeds for him. We try not to appear angry at his misanthropy and his unnaturalness. But we feel that he is more often in the wrong than in the right. We see in him a man who loved the truth passionately and who almost invariably grasped at falsehood. He is surpassed intellectually by most of the great sceptics of France in the seventeenth century. Their views have received additional support by the latest scientific discoveries and many of these men are undeservedly forgotten, overshadowed by Pascal. He is not one of the real glories of French literature. The prose literature of France in the seventeenth and eighteenth centuries can show us greater thinkers.

Pascal's *Thoughts* is another one of those classics whose fame declined in the eighteenth century. It would be well for the progress of thought that his sun should set again. The modern apologists for dogma who are not honest thinkers draw largely from the *Thoughts*. Pascal after Darwin sounds anomalous. The man who bases philosophy on revelation and morality on asceticism is antiquated for modern times. Yet much can be extracted from his works to give him a fairly respectable though not a very high place in the temple of fame. Probably he deserves to be better known for his mathematical and scientific discoveries than for his religious apologies. The laws he discovered about atmospheric pressure and the equilibrium of fluids are still true; his Christian evidence is obsolete. The world will always regret that a precocious mathematical genius who composed a treatise on Conic Sections before he was 16 years old should have stepped out into an abyss of superstition and dogma.

What is surprising is the hold he has had on modern writers like St. Beuve and Pater. Even Nietzsche loved him. Nietzsche called him the " only *logical* Christian " and blamed his ruin on Christianity. But George Moore was bold enough to write: " *Les Pensees* could appear to me only as infinitely childish; the form is no doubt superb, but tiresome and sterile to one of such modern and exotic taste as myself."

APPENDIX

Adverse Views on Dante

Landor said: " It would be difficult to form an idea of a poem into which so many personages are introduced containing so few delineations of character, so few touches that excite sympathy, so few elementary signs for our instruction, so few topics for our delight, so few excursions for our recreation."

Emerson's biographer, Cabot, reports the opinion of the sage of Concord on the Florentine poet as follows: " A man to put in a museum, but not in your house: another Zerah Colburn; a prodigy of imaginative function, executive rather than contemplative or wise." (Zerah Colburn was a mathematical prodigy.)

Oliver Goldsmith said: " He shows a strange mixture of good sense and absurdity. The truth is, he owes most of his reputation to the obscurity of the times in which he lived. As in the land of Benim a man may pass as a prodigy of parts who can read, so in an age of barbarity a small degree of excellence secures success."

Strindberg in his autobiography speaks thus of the *Divine Comedy:* " Even with regard to its own time the work is not an epoch-making one; it is not in advance of its period, but belongs strictly to it, or rather lags behind it. It is a linguistic monument for Italy, nothing more . . . . it is too insignificant to be regarded as a link in the development of culture."

Voltaire in his correspondence writes as follows: " There are to be found among us, in the eighteenth century, people who force themselves to admire feats of imagination as stupidly extravagant and as barbarous as this."

Goethe registered this opinion in his *Italian Travels:* "The hell was to me altogether horrible, the purgatory neither one thing nor another, and the paradise dreadfully slow."

Leigh Hunt says: "Such a vision as that of his poem (in a theological point of view) seems no better than the dream of a hypochondriacal savage and his nutshell a rottenness to be spit out of the mouth."

Lamartine, the French poet, finds in Dante "a coarse triviality which descends to cynicism of expression and debauchery of image, a quintessence of scholastic theology which rises to vaporisation of the idea, finally to say everything in a word, a great man and a bad book."

To Horace Walpole "Dante was extravagant, absurd, disgusting; in short, a Methodist parson in Bedlam."

To Nietzsche Dante was "the hyena poetising in tombs."

Howard Candler in an article called "The Black-Washing of Dante" published in the *Nineteenth Century* says: "And so we leave him, the mighty personification of medievalism and scholasticism, the last apostle of unquestioning faith in the figments of tradition, without a single lesson for the future, and utterly unmoved by any free breath of that sceptical spirit which ushered in the Reformation and the modern world."

ADVERSE VIEWS ON MILTON

Carlyle is quoted in *Cunningham's Diary* as follows:

"*Paradise Lost* is absurd. I never could take to it all—though now and again clouds of splendor rolled in upon the scene."

Goethe's verdict appears in a letter to Schiller dated July 31, 1799:

" The subject is detestable, outwardly plausible and inwardly worm-eaten and hollow. With the exception of the few natural and vigorous motives there are a number which are lame and false, and which offend one."

Poe wrote: " The fact is, if the *Paradise Lost* were written to-day (assuming that it had never been written when it was), not even its eminent, although overestimated merits, would counterbalance, either in the public view, or in the opinion of any critic at once intelligent and honest, the multitudinous incongruities that are part and parcel of its plot."

Samuel Johnson spoke for many people when he said: " *Paradise Lost* is one of the books which the reader admires and lays down, and forgets to take up again. No one ever wished it longer than it is. Its perusal is a duty rather than a pleasure."

Of course Walt Whitman would hardly care for the poem. He said to Horace Traubel " . . . . even as a story it enlists little of my attention: he seems to me like a bird—soaring yet overweighted: dragged down as if hindered—too greatly hindered: a lamb in its beak: its flight not graceful, powerful, beautiful, satisfying, like the gulls we see on the Delaware in midwinter."

Voltaire in his novel *Candide* has a character who speaks thus of the renowned work: " This obscure poem, fantastic and revolting, was despised when it first made its appearance, and I treat it now as it was treated in his (Milton's) own country by his own generation."

Scherer, the noted French critic, exclaimed: " *Paradise Lost* is an unreal poem, a grotesque poem, a tiresome poem. There is not one reader in a hundred who can read books nine and ten without a smile, or books eleven and twelve without a yawn. The thing does not hold together: it is a pyramid balanced on its apex, the most terrible of problems solved by the most childish of means."

A still greater critic, Taine, said: " He gives us correct solemn discourse, and gives us nothing more; his characters are speeches, and in their sentiments we find only heaps of puerilities and contradictions."

The author of *Omar Khayam*, Fitzgerald, remarked: " I never could read ten lines of *Paradise Lost* without stumbling at some pedantry that tipped me at once out of paradise or even hell into the schoolroom worse than either."

Adverse Views on Bunyan

Poe wrote: " That the *Pilgrim's Progress* is a ludicrously overrated book, owing its seeming popularity to one or two of those accidents in critical literature which by the critical are sufficiently well understood, is a matter upon which no two thinking people disagree."

The late Samuel Butler, whom Shaw rediscovered for us, said: " The *Pilgrim's Progress* consists mainly of a series of infamous libels upon life and things; it is a blasphemy against certain fundamental ideas of right and wrong which our consciences most instinctly approve .... There is no conception of the faith that a man should do his duty cheerfully, with all his might, though, as far as he can see, he will never be paid directly or indirectly either here or hereafter."

Taine wrote in a letter as follows, about the celebrated allegory: " It is a nursery tale, a blood-curdling allegory, showing the terrible inner mind of one of those fanatics;

groans, invasions of the spirit, the belief in damnation, visions of the devil, scruples, etc."

Richard Dowling in a book called *Ignorant Essays* says: "The whole thing is grotesquely absurd and impossible to imagine. There is no sobriety in it; no sobriety of keeping in it; and no matter how wild the effort or vision of imagination may be there must always be sobriety of keeping in it, or it is delirium, not imagination, disease, not inspiration. As far as I can see there is no trace of imagination or even fancy in the *Pilgrim's Progress*. The story never happened at all. It is a horrible attempt to tinkerize the Bible."

Francis Thompson, the poet, reviewing Dowling's book sympathetically, speaks thus of the allegory: "We have searched the book in vain for a single scene with a single master-touch of delineation; and the result has been thoroughly to convince us that the man was incapable of such a thing, he *knew* himself incapable, and therefore instinctively shirked description."